50 United Kingdom Ice Cream Recipes for Home

By: Kelly Johnson

Table of Contents

- Vanilla Bean Ice Cream
- Strawberry Ice Cream
- Chocolate Ice Cream
- Mint Chocolate Chip Ice Cream
- Raspberry Ripple Ice Cream
- Clotted Cream Ice Cream
- Eton Mess Ice Cream
- Sticky Toffee Pudding Ice Cream
- Banoffee Pie Ice Cream
- Honeycomb Ice Cream
- Rhubarb and Custard Ice Cream
- Lemon Curd Ice Cream
- Blackberry Ice Cream
- Gingerbread Ice Cream
- Cherry Bakewell Ice Cream
- Marmalade Ice Cream
- Peach Melba Ice Cream
- Blackcurrant Ice Cream
- Apple Crumble Ice Cream
- Lavender and Honey Ice Cream
- Spotted Dick Ice Cream
- Earl Grey Tea Ice Cream
- Pimm's Ice Cream
- Salted Caramel Ice Cream
- Irish Cream Liqueur Ice Cream
- Whisky and Ginger Ice Cream
- Gooseberry Ice Cream
- Mulled Wine Ice Cream
- Lemon and Elderflower Ice Cream
- Cranachan Ice Cream
- Pumpkin Spice Ice Cream
- Treacle Tart Ice Cream
- Coffee and Walnut Ice Cream
- Turkish Delight Ice Cream
- Matcha Green Tea Ice Cream

- Cardamom and Saffron Ice Cream
- Cucumber and Mint Ice Cream
- Pear and Blue Cheese Ice Cream
- Beetroot and Chocolate Ice Cream
- Fig and Honey Ice Cream
- Toasted Coconut Ice Cream
- Brown Bread Ice Cream
- Chai Spiced Ice Cream
- Sloe Gin Ice Cream
- Pistachio Ice Cream
- Christmas Pudding Ice Cream
- Bubblegum Ice Cream
- Rum and Raisin Ice Cream
- Rocky Road Ice Cream
- Peanut Butter and Jelly Ice Cream

Vanilla Bean Ice Cream

Ingredients:

- 2 cups (480 ml) heavy cream
- 1 cup (240 ml) whole milk
- 3/4 cup (150 g) granulated sugar
- 1 vanilla bean
- 5 large egg yolks
- 1 teaspoon pure vanilla extract

Instructions:

1. **Prepare the Vanilla Bean:**
   - Slice the vanilla bean lengthwise and scrape out the seeds using the back of a knife. Set aside.
2. **Heat the Cream and Milk:**
   - In a medium saucepan, combine the heavy cream, whole milk, sugar, and the scraped vanilla bean seeds along with the pod.
   - Heat the mixture over medium heat, stirring occasionally, until it begins to steam and tiny bubbles form around the edges. Do not let it boil.
   - Remove from heat and let the mixture steep for about 30 minutes to infuse the vanilla flavor.
3. **Prepare the Egg Yolks:**
   - In a separate bowl, whisk the egg yolks until they are pale and slightly thickened.
4. **Temper the Egg Yolks:**
   - Gradually whisk about 1/2 cup of the warm cream mixture into the egg yolks to temper them. This prevents the yolks from curdling when added to the hot mixture.
   - Slowly pour the tempered egg yolk mixture back into the saucepan with the remaining cream mixture, stirring constantly.
5. **Cook the Custard:**
   - Return the saucepan to the stove over medium-low heat. Cook the mixture, stirring constantly with a wooden spoon or heatproof spatula, until it thickens and coats the back of the spoon. This should take about 5-7 minutes. Do not let it boil.
   - The custard is ready when it reaches about 170-175°F (77-80°C) on a kitchen thermometer.
6. **Strain and Cool:**

- Remove the custard from heat and strain it through a fine-mesh sieve into a clean bowl. This removes the vanilla pod and any cooked egg bits.
- Stir in the pure vanilla extract.
- Let the custard cool to room temperature, then cover and refrigerate for at least 4 hours or overnight. The custard should be thoroughly chilled before churning.

7. **Churn the Ice Cream:**
   - Once the custard is chilled, pour it into your ice cream maker and churn according to the manufacturer's instructions. This usually takes about 20-25 minutes.
8. **Freeze the Ice Cream:**
   - Transfer the churned ice cream to an airtight container and freeze for at least 4 hours or until firm.
9. **Serve:**
   - Scoop and enjoy your homemade vanilla bean ice cream!

Feel free to customize this basic vanilla bean ice cream recipe by adding mix-ins like chocolate chips, caramel swirls, or fruit compote. Enjoy!

Strawberry Ice Cream

Ingredients:

- 1 pound (450 g) fresh strawberries, hulled and sliced
- 3/4 cup (150 g) granulated sugar, divided
- 2 teaspoons lemon juice
- 2 cups (480 ml) heavy cream
- 1 cup (240 ml) whole milk
- 5 large egg yolks
- 1 teaspoon pure vanilla extract

Instructions:

1. **Prepare the Strawberries:**
   - In a medium bowl, combine the sliced strawberries, 1/4 cup (50 g) of sugar, and lemon juice.
   - Let the mixture sit for about 30 minutes, stirring occasionally, until the strawberries release their juices.
2. **Puree the Strawberries:**
   - Using a blender or food processor, puree the strawberries until smooth.
   - If you prefer a chunkier texture, reserve some of the strawberries and chop them finely to mix in later.
3. **Heat the Cream and Milk:**
   - In a medium saucepan, combine the heavy cream, whole milk, and the remaining 1/2 cup (100 g) of sugar.
   - Heat the mixture over medium heat, stirring occasionally, until it begins to steam and tiny bubbles form around the edges. Do not let it boil.
4. **Prepare the Egg Yolks:**
   - In a separate bowl, whisk the egg yolks until they are pale and slightly thickened.
5. **Temper the Egg Yolks:**
   - Gradually whisk about 1/2 cup of the warm cream mixture into the egg yolks to temper them. This prevents the yolks from curdling when added to the hot mixture.
   - Slowly pour the tempered egg yolk mixture back into the saucepan with the remaining cream mixture, stirring constantly.
6. **Cook the Custard:**
   - Return the saucepan to the stove over medium-low heat. Cook the mixture, stirring constantly with a wooden spoon or heatproof spatula, until it

thickens and coats the back of the spoon. This should take about 5-7 minutes. Do not let it boil.
   - The custard is ready when it reaches about 170-175°F (77-80°C) on a kitchen thermometer.
7. **Combine Custard and Strawberries:**
   - Remove the custard from heat and strain it through a fine-mesh sieve into a clean bowl to remove any cooked egg bits.
   - Stir in the pureed strawberries and vanilla extract.
   - Let the mixture cool to room temperature, then cover and refrigerate for at least 4 hours or overnight. The custard should be thoroughly chilled before churning.
8. **Churn the Ice Cream:**
   - Once the custard is chilled, pour it into your ice cream maker and churn according to the manufacturer's instructions. This usually takes about 20-25 minutes.
9. **Freeze the Ice Cream:**
   - Transfer the churned ice cream to an airtight container and freeze for at least 4 hours or until firm.
10. **Serve:**
    - Scoop and enjoy your homemade strawberry ice cream!

Feel free to add mix-ins like chocolate chips or swirl in some strawberry jam for extra flavor. Enjoy!

Chocolate Ice Cream

Ingredients:

- 2 cups (480 ml) heavy cream
- 1 cup (240 ml) whole milk
- 3/4 cup (150 g) granulated sugar
- 1/2 cup (50 g) unsweetened cocoa powder
- 5 large egg yolks
- 6 oz (170 g) bittersweet or semisweet chocolate, finely chopped
- 1 teaspoon pure vanilla extract
- Pinch of salt

Instructions:

1. **Heat the Cream and Milk:**
    - In a medium saucepan, combine the heavy cream, whole milk, and 1/2 cup (100 g) of the sugar.
    - Heat the mixture over medium heat, stirring occasionally, until it begins to steam and tiny bubbles form around the edges. Do not let it boil.
2. **Prepare the Cocoa Mixture:**
    - In a small bowl, whisk together the cocoa powder and remaining 1/4 cup (50 g) of sugar.
    - Gradually whisk the cocoa mixture into the hot cream mixture until smooth.
3. **Melt the Chocolate:**
    - Add the chopped chocolate to the hot cream mixture and stir until completely melted and smooth.
4. **Prepare the Egg Yolks:**
    - In a separate bowl, whisk the egg yolks until they are pale and slightly thickened.
5. **Temper the Egg Yolks:**
    - Gradually whisk about 1/2 cup of the warm chocolate mixture into the egg yolks to temper them. This prevents the yolks from curdling when added to the hot mixture.
    - Slowly pour the tempered egg yolk mixture back into the saucepan with the remaining chocolate mixture, stirring constantly.
6. **Cook the Custard:**
    - Return the saucepan to the stove over medium-low heat. Cook the mixture, stirring constantly with a wooden spoon or heatproof spatula, until it

thickens and coats the back of the spoon. This should take about 5-7 minutes. Do not let it boil.
    - The custard is ready when it reaches about 170-175°F (77-80°C) on a kitchen thermometer.
7. **Strain and Cool:**
    - Remove the custard from heat and strain it through a fine-mesh sieve into a clean bowl to remove any cooked egg bits.
    - Stir in the vanilla extract and a pinch of salt.
    - Let the custard cool to room temperature, then cover and refrigerate for at least 4 hours or overnight. The custard should be thoroughly chilled before churning.
8. **Churn the Ice Cream:**
    - Once the custard is chilled, pour it into your ice cream maker and churn according to the manufacturer's instructions. This usually takes about 20-25 minutes.
9. **Freeze the Ice Cream:**
    - Transfer the churned ice cream to an airtight container and freeze for at least 4 hours or until firm.
10. **Serve:**
    - Scoop and enjoy your homemade chocolate ice cream!

Feel free to add mix-ins like chocolate chips, nuts, or marshmallows for extra texture and flavor. Enjoy!

Mint Chocolate Chip Ice Cream

Ingredients:

- 2 cups (480 ml) heavy cream
- 1 cup (240 ml) whole milk
- 3/4 cup (150 g) granulated sugar
- 5 large egg yolks
- 1 teaspoon pure vanilla extract
- 2 teaspoons peppermint extract
- 1-2 drops green food coloring (optional)
- 1 cup (175 g) mini chocolate chips or finely chopped chocolate

Instructions:

1. **Heat the Cream and Milk:**
    - In a medium saucepan, combine the heavy cream, whole milk, and sugar.
    - Heat the mixture over medium heat, stirring occasionally, until it begins to steam and tiny bubbles form around the edges. Do not let it boil.
2. **Prepare the Egg Yolks:**
    - In a separate bowl, whisk the egg yolks until they are pale and slightly thickened.
3. **Temper the Egg Yolks:**
    - Gradually whisk about 1/2 cup of the warm cream mixture into the egg yolks to temper them. This prevents the yolks from curdling when added to the hot mixture.
    - Slowly pour the tempered egg yolk mixture back into the saucepan with the remaining cream mixture, stirring constantly.
4. **Cook the Custard:**
    - Return the saucepan to the stove over medium-low heat. Cook the mixture, stirring constantly with a wooden spoon or heatproof spatula, until it thickens and coats the back of the spoon. This should take about 5-7 minutes. Do not let it boil.
    - The custard is ready when it reaches about 170-175°F (77-80°C) on a kitchen thermometer.
5. **Strain and Cool:**
    - Remove the custard from heat and strain it through a fine-mesh sieve into a clean bowl to remove any cooked egg bits.
    - Stir in the vanilla extract, peppermint extract, and green food coloring (if using).

- Let the custard cool to room temperature, then cover and refrigerate for at least 4 hours or overnight. The custard should be thoroughly chilled before churning.
6. **Churn the Ice Cream:**
    - Once the custard is chilled, pour it into your ice cream maker and churn according to the manufacturer's instructions. This usually takes about 20-25 minutes.
    - During the last few minutes of churning, add the mini chocolate chips or finely chopped chocolate.
7. **Freeze the Ice Cream:**
    - Transfer the churned ice cream to an airtight container and freeze for at least 4 hours or until firm.
8. **Serve:**
    - Scoop and enjoy your homemade mint chocolate chip ice cream!

Feel free to adjust the amount of peppermint extract to taste and enjoy the refreshing flavor of mint combined with the delightful crunch of chocolate chips. Enjoy!

Raspberry Ripple Ice Cream

Ingredients:

For the Raspberry Sauce:

- 2 cups (250 g) fresh or frozen raspberries
- 1/2 cup (100 g) granulated sugar
- 1 tablespoon lemon juice

For the Ice Cream Base:

- 2 cups (480 ml) heavy cream
- 1 cup (240 ml) whole milk
- 3/4 cup (150 g) granulated sugar
- 1 vanilla bean (or 2 teaspoons pure vanilla extract)
- 5 large egg yolks

Instructions:

1. **Prepare the Raspberry Sauce:**
    - In a medium saucepan, combine the raspberries, sugar, and lemon juice.
    - Cook over medium heat, stirring occasionally, until the raspberries break down and the mixture thickens, about 10-15 minutes.
    - Remove from heat and strain through a fine-mesh sieve to remove the seeds. Let the sauce cool to room temperature, then refrigerate until ready to use.
2. **Heat the Cream and Milk:**
    - In a medium saucepan, combine the heavy cream, whole milk, and sugar.
    - If using a vanilla bean, split it lengthwise, scrape out the seeds, and add both the seeds and the pod to the saucepan.
    - Heat the mixture over medium heat, stirring occasionally, until it begins to steam and tiny bubbles form around the edges. Do not let it boil.
3. **Prepare the Egg Yolks:**
    - In a separate bowl, whisk the egg yolks until they are pale and slightly thickened.
4. **Temper the Egg Yolks:**
    - Gradually whisk about 1/2 cup of the warm cream mixture into the egg yolks to temper them. This prevents the yolks from curdling when added to the hot mixture.

- Slowly pour the tempered egg yolk mixture back into the saucepan with the remaining cream mixture, stirring constantly.

5. **Cook the Custard:**
   - Return the saucepan to the stove over medium-low heat. Cook the mixture, stirring constantly with a wooden spoon or heatproof spatula, until it thickens and coats the back of the spoon. This should take about 5-7 minutes. Do not let it boil.
   - The custard is ready when it reaches about 170-175°F (77-80°C) on a kitchen thermometer.

6. **Strain and Cool:**
   - Remove the custard from heat and strain it through a fine-mesh sieve into a clean bowl to remove any cooked egg bits and the vanilla bean pod if used.
   - If using vanilla extract, stir it in now.
   - Let the custard cool to room temperature, then cover and refrigerate for at least 4 hours or overnight. The custard should be thoroughly chilled before churning.

7. **Churn the Ice Cream:**
   - Once the custard is chilled, pour it into your ice cream maker and churn according to the manufacturer's instructions. This usually takes about 20-25 minutes.

8. **Ripple the Raspberry Sauce:**
   - Transfer half of the churned ice cream to an airtight container. Drizzle half of the raspberry sauce over the ice cream.
   - Use a knife or skewer to gently swirl the sauce through the ice cream.
   - Repeat with the remaining ice cream and raspberry sauce.

9. **Freeze the Ice Cream:**
   - Cover the container and freeze for at least 4 hours or until firm.

10. **Serve:**
    - Scoop and enjoy your homemade raspberry ripple ice cream!

Enjoy the delightful contrast of creamy vanilla ice cream and tangy raspberry swirls!

Clotted Cream Ice Cream

Ingredients:

- 1 1/2 cups (360 ml) heavy cream
- 1 cup (240 ml) whole milk
- 1 cup (240 g) clotted cream
- 3/4 cup (150 g) granulated sugar
- 5 large egg yolks
- 1 teaspoon pure vanilla extract

Instructions:

1. **Heat the Cream and Milk:**
    - In a medium saucepan, combine the heavy cream, whole milk, and sugar.
    - Heat the mixture over medium heat, stirring occasionally, until it begins to steam and tiny bubbles form around the edges. Do not let it boil.
2. **Prepare the Egg Yolks:**
    - In a separate bowl, whisk the egg yolks until they are pale and slightly thickened.
3. **Temper the Egg Yolks:**
    - Gradually whisk about 1/2 cup of the warm cream mixture into the egg yolks to temper them. This prevents the yolks from curdling when added to the hot mixture.
    - Slowly pour the tempered egg yolk mixture back into the saucepan with the remaining cream mixture, stirring constantly.
4. **Cook the Custard:**
    - Return the saucepan to the stove over medium-low heat. Cook the mixture, stirring constantly with a wooden spoon or heatproof spatula, until it thickens and coats the back of the spoon. This should take about 5-7 minutes. Do not let it boil.
    - The custard is ready when it reaches about 170-175°F (77-80°C) on a kitchen thermometer.
5. **Strain and Cool:**
    - Remove the custard from heat and strain it through a fine-mesh sieve into a clean bowl to remove any cooked egg bits.
    - Stir in the vanilla extract.
    - Let the custard cool to room temperature, then cover and refrigerate for at least 4 hours or overnight. The custard should be thoroughly chilled before churning.

6. **Combine with Clotted Cream:**
    - Once the custard is chilled, gently whisk in the clotted cream until fully incorporated.
7. **Churn the Ice Cream:**
    - Pour the mixture into your ice cream maker and churn according to the manufacturer's instructions. This usually takes about 20-25 minutes.
8. **Freeze the Ice Cream:**
    - Transfer the churned ice cream to an airtight container and freeze for at least 4 hours or until firm.
9. **Serve:**
    - Scoop and enjoy your homemade clotted cream ice cream!

This recipe captures the rich and indulgent flavor of clotted cream in a smooth and creamy ice cream. Enjoy!

Eton Mess Ice Cream

Ingredients:

For the Meringue:

- 2 large egg whites
- 1/2 cup (100 g) granulated sugar

For the Strawberry Sauce:

- 1 pound (450 g) fresh strawberries, hulled and sliced
- 1/4 cup (50 g) granulated sugar
- 1 tablespoon lemon juice

For the Ice Cream Base:

- 2 cups (480 ml) heavy cream
- 1 cup (240 ml) whole milk
- 3/4 cup (150 g) granulated sugar
- 1 vanilla bean (or 2 teaspoons pure vanilla extract)
- 5 large egg yolks

Instructions:

1. **Prepare the Meringue:**
    - Preheat your oven to 250°F (120°C) and line a baking sheet with parchment paper.
    - In a clean, dry bowl, beat the egg whites until they form soft peaks.
    - Gradually add the sugar, continuing to beat until the mixture forms stiff, glossy peaks.
    - Spoon or pipe the meringue onto the prepared baking sheet in small mounds.
    - Bake for about 1-1.5 hours, or until the meringues are crisp and dry. Turn off the oven and let them cool completely in the oven. Once cool, break into small pieces and set aside.
2. **Prepare the Strawberry Sauce:**
    - In a medium saucepan, combine the strawberries, sugar, and lemon juice.
    - Cook over medium heat, stirring occasionally, until the strawberries break down and the mixture thickens, about 10-15 minutes.

- Remove from heat and let the sauce cool to room temperature, then refrigerate until ready to use.
3. **Heat the Cream and Milk:**
    - In a medium saucepan, combine the heavy cream, whole milk, and sugar.
    - If using a vanilla bean, split it lengthwise, scrape out the seeds, and add both the seeds and the pod to the saucepan.
    - Heat the mixture over medium heat, stirring occasionally, until it begins to steam and tiny bubbles form around the edges. Do not let it boil.
4. **Prepare the Egg Yolks:**
    - In a separate bowl, whisk the egg yolks until they are pale and slightly thickened.
5. **Temper the Egg Yolks:**
    - Gradually whisk about 1/2 cup of the warm cream mixture into the egg yolks to temper them. This prevents the yolks from curdling when added to the hot mixture.
    - Slowly pour the tempered egg yolk mixture back into the saucepan with the remaining cream mixture, stirring constantly.
6. **Cook the Custard:**
    - Return the saucepan to the stove over medium-low heat. Cook the mixture, stirring constantly with a wooden spoon or heatproof spatula, until it thickens and coats the back of the spoon. This should take about 5-7 minutes. Do not let it boil.
    - The custard is ready when it reaches about 170-175°F (77-80°C) on a kitchen thermometer.
7. **Strain and Cool:**
    - Remove the custard from heat and strain it through a fine-mesh sieve into a clean bowl to remove any cooked egg bits and the vanilla bean pod if used.
    - If using vanilla extract, stir it in now.
    - Let the custard cool to room temperature, then cover and refrigerate for at least 4 hours or overnight. The custard should be thoroughly chilled before churning.
8. **Churn the Ice Cream:**
    - Once the custard is chilled, pour it into your ice cream maker and churn according to the manufacturer's instructions. This usually takes about 20-25 minutes.
9. **Combine with Meringue and Strawberry Sauce:**

- Transfer half of the churned ice cream to an airtight container. Gently fold in half of the meringue pieces and drizzle half of the strawberry sauce over the ice cream.
- Use a knife or skewer to gently swirl the sauce through the ice cream.
- Repeat with the remaining ice cream, meringue, and strawberry sauce.

10. **Freeze the Ice Cream:**
    - Cover the container and freeze for at least 4 hours or until firm.
11. **Serve:**
    - Scoop and enjoy your homemade Eton Mess ice cream!

This ice cream combines the classic flavors of Eton Mess with creamy vanilla ice cream, making it a delightful and refreshing dessert. Enjoy!

Sticky Toffee Pudding Ice Cream

Ingredients:

For the Sticky Toffee Pudding:

- 1 cup (150 g) chopped dates
- 3/4 cup (180 ml) boiling water
- 1 teaspoon baking soda
- 1/2 cup (100 g) granulated sugar
- 1/2 cup (100 g) brown sugar, packed
- 1 1/4 cups (160 g) all-purpose flour
- 1/2 teaspoon baking powder
- 1/4 teaspoon salt
- 1/4 cup (60 g) unsalted butter, softened
- 2 large eggs
- 1 teaspoon vanilla extract

For the Toffee Sauce:

- 1/2 cup (100 g) brown sugar, packed
- 1/2 cup (120 ml) heavy cream
- 1/4 cup (60 g) unsalted butter
- 1 teaspoon vanilla extract
- Pinch of salt

For the Ice Cream Base:

- 2 cups (480 ml) heavy cream
- 1 cup (240 ml) whole milk
- 3/4 cup (150 g) granulated sugar
- 5 large egg yolks
- 1 teaspoon vanilla extract

Instructions:

1. **Prepare the Sticky Toffee Pudding:**
    - Preheat your oven to 350°F (175°C) and grease a small baking dish.
    - In a bowl, combine the chopped dates and boiling water. Stir in the baking soda and let sit for 15 minutes to soften the dates.
    - In a separate bowl, whisk together the flour, baking powder, and salt.

- In a large bowl, cream together the softened butter, granulated sugar, and brown sugar until light and fluffy.
- Beat in the eggs one at a time, then stir in the vanilla extract.
- Gradually add the flour mixture to the butter mixture, mixing just until combined.
- Fold in the date mixture, including any soaking liquid.
- Pour the batter into the prepared baking dish and bake for 25-30 minutes, or until a toothpick inserted into the center comes out clean.
- Allow the pudding to cool, then cut it into small pieces.

2. **Prepare the Toffee Sauce:**
    - In a medium saucepan, combine the brown sugar, heavy cream, and butter.
    - Cook over medium heat, stirring constantly, until the mixture comes to a boil.
    - Reduce the heat and simmer for about 3-4 minutes, until the sauce thickens.
    - Remove from heat and stir in the vanilla extract and a pinch of salt. Let cool to room temperature.

3. **Prepare the Ice Cream Base:**
    - In a medium saucepan, combine the heavy cream, whole milk, and granulated sugar.
    - Heat the mixture over medium heat, stirring occasionally, until it begins to steam and tiny bubbles form around the edges. Do not let it boil.
    - In a separate bowl, whisk the egg yolks until they are pale and slightly thickened.
    - Gradually whisk about 1/2 cup of the warm cream mixture into the egg yolks to temper them.
    - Slowly pour the tempered egg yolk mixture back into the saucepan with the remaining cream mixture, stirring constantly.
    - Return the saucepan to the stove over medium-low heat. Cook the mixture, stirring constantly, until it thickens and coats the back of the spoon. This should take about 5-7 minutes.
    - Remove from heat and strain the custard through a fine-mesh sieve into a clean bowl to remove any cooked egg bits.
    - Stir in the vanilla extract and let the custard cool to room temperature, then cover and refrigerate for at least 4 hours or overnight.

4. **Churn the Ice Cream:**
    - Once the custard is chilled, pour it into your ice cream maker and churn according to the manufacturer's instructions. This usually takes about 20-25 minutes.

5. **Combine the Elements:**
    - Transfer half of the churned ice cream to an airtight container.
    - Gently fold in pieces of sticky toffee pudding and drizzle some of the toffee sauce over the ice cream.
    - Use a knife or skewer to swirl the sauce through the ice cream.
    - Repeat with the remaining ice cream, pudding pieces, and toffee sauce.
6. **Freeze the Ice Cream:**
    - Cover the container and freeze for at least 4 hours or until firm.
7. **Serve:**
    - Scoop and enjoy your homemade sticky toffee pudding ice cream!

Enjoy the rich and decadent flavors of sticky toffee pudding in a creamy ice cream form.

Banoffee Pie Ice Cream

Ingredients:

For the Banana Layer:

- 3 ripe bananas, mashed
- 2 tablespoons lemon juice

For the Toffee Sauce:

- 1/2 cup (100 g) brown sugar, packed
- 1/2 cup (120 ml) heavy cream
- 1/4 cup (60 g) unsalted butter
- 1 teaspoon vanilla extract
- Pinch of salt

For the Ice Cream Base:

- 2 cups (480 ml) heavy cream
- 1 cup (240 ml) whole milk
- 3/4 cup (150 g) granulated sugar
- 5 large egg yolks
- 1 teaspoon vanilla extract

For the Graham Cracker Crumble:

- 1 cup (100 g) graham cracker crumbs
- 1/4 cup (50 g) granulated sugar
- 1/4 cup (60 g) unsalted butter, melted

Instructions:

1. **Prepare the Banana Layer:**
    - In a bowl, mash the bananas and stir in the lemon juice to prevent browning. Set aside.
2. **Prepare the Toffee Sauce:**
    - In a medium saucepan, combine the brown sugar, heavy cream, and butter.
    - Cook over medium heat, stirring constantly, until the mixture comes to a boil.
    - Reduce the heat and simmer for about 3-4 minutes, until the sauce thickens.

- Remove from heat and stir in the vanilla extract and a pinch of salt. Let cool to room temperature.

3. **Prepare the Ice Cream Base:**
   - In a medium saucepan, combine the heavy cream, whole milk, and granulated sugar.
   - Heat the mixture over medium heat, stirring occasionally, until it begins to steam and tiny bubbles form around the edges. Do not let it boil.
   - In a separate bowl, whisk the egg yolks until they are pale and slightly thickened.
   - Gradually whisk about 1/2 cup of the warm cream mixture into the egg yolks to temper them.
   - Slowly pour the tempered egg yolk mixture back into the saucepan with the remaining cream mixture, stirring constantly.
   - Return the saucepan to the stove over medium-low heat. Cook the mixture, stirring constantly, until it thickens and coats the back of the spoon. This should take about 5-7 minutes.
   - Remove from heat and strain the custard through a fine-mesh sieve into a clean bowl to remove any cooked egg bits.
   - Stir in the vanilla extract and let the custard cool to room temperature, then cover and refrigerate for at least 4 hours or overnight.

4. **Prepare the Graham Cracker Crumble:**
   - Preheat your oven to 350°F (175°C) and line a baking sheet with parchment paper.
   - In a bowl, combine the graham cracker crumbs, granulated sugar, and melted butter.
   - Spread the mixture evenly on the prepared baking sheet and bake for about 10 minutes, or until golden brown. Let cool completely.

5. **Churn the Ice Cream:**
   - Once the custard is chilled, pour it into your ice cream maker and churn according to the manufacturer's instructions. This usually takes about 20-25 minutes.
   - During the last few minutes of churning, add the mashed bananas to the ice cream mixture.

6. **Combine the Elements:**
   - Transfer half of the churned ice cream to an airtight container.
   - Drizzle some of the toffee sauce over the ice cream and sprinkle with some of the graham cracker crumble.
   - Use a knife or skewer to gently swirl the sauce and crumbs through the ice cream.

- Repeat with the remaining ice cream, toffee sauce, and graham cracker crumble.
7. **Freeze the Ice Cream:**
    - Cover the container and freeze for at least 4 hours or until firm.
8. **Serve:**
    - Scoop and enjoy your homemade banoffee pie ice cream!

This ice cream captures the delightful flavors of a classic banoffee pie with creamy banana, rich toffee, and crunchy graham cracker crumble. Enjoy!

Honeycomb Ice Cream

Ingredients:

For the Honeycomb Candy:

- 1 cup (200 g) granulated sugar
- 1/4 cup (60 ml) honey
- 1/4 cup (60 ml) water
- 1 tablespoon baking soda

For the Ice Cream Base:

- 2 cups (480 ml) heavy cream
- 1 cup (240 ml) whole milk
- 3/4 cup (150 g) granulated sugar
- 5 large egg yolks
- 1 teaspoon vanilla extract

Instructions:

1. **Prepare the Honeycomb Candy:**
   - Line a baking sheet with parchment paper or a silicone baking mat.
   - In a medium saucepan, combine the sugar, honey, and water over medium heat.
   - Stir until the sugar dissolves, then let the mixture come to a boil without stirring.
   - Cook until it reaches 300°F (150°C) on a candy thermometer, or until it turns a deep amber color (this should take about 5-7 minutes).
   - Remove from heat and quickly whisk in the baking soda until well combined. Be cautious as the mixture will bubble up vigorously.
   - Immediately pour the mixture onto the prepared baking sheet. Let it cool and harden completely, then break into small pieces.
2. **Prepare the Ice Cream Base:**
   - In a medium saucepan, combine the heavy cream, whole milk, and granulated sugar.
   - Heat the mixture over medium heat, stirring occasionally, until it begins to steam and tiny bubbles form around the edges. Do not let it boil.
   - In a separate bowl, whisk the egg yolks until they are pale and slightly thickened.

- Gradually whisk about 1/2 cup of the warm cream mixture into the egg yolks to temper them.
- Slowly pour the tempered egg yolk mixture back into the saucepan with the remaining cream mixture, stirring constantly.
- Return the saucepan to the stove over medium-low heat. Cook the mixture, stirring constantly, until it thickens and coats the back of the spoon. This should take about 5-7 minutes.
- Remove from heat and strain the custard through a fine-mesh sieve into a clean bowl to remove any cooked egg bits.
- Stir in the vanilla extract and let the custard cool to room temperature, then cover and refrigerate for at least 4 hours or overnight.

3. **Churn the Ice Cream:**
    - Once the custard is chilled, pour it into your ice cream maker and churn according to the manufacturer's instructions. This usually takes about 20-25 minutes.
4. **Combine with Honeycomb Pieces:**
    - During the last few minutes of churning, add the broken honeycomb candy pieces to the ice cream and continue churning until evenly distributed.
5. **Freeze the Ice Cream:**
    - Transfer the churned ice cream to an airtight container and freeze for at least 4 hours or until firm.
6. **Serve:**
    - Scoop and enjoy your homemade honeycomb ice cream!

This recipe combines creamy ice cream with crunchy, sweet honeycomb candy for a delightful treat. Enjoy the contrast of textures and flavors!

Rhubarb and Custard Ice Cream

Ingredients:

For the Rhubarb Compote:

- 3 cups (about 400g) fresh rhubarb, chopped into 1-inch pieces
- 1/2 cup (100g) granulated sugar
- 1/4 cup (60ml) water

For the Custard Base:

- 2 cups (480ml) heavy cream
- 1 cup (240ml) whole milk
- 3/4 cup (150g) granulated sugar
- 5 large egg yolks
- 1 teaspoon vanilla extract

Instructions:

1. **Prepare the Rhubarb Compote:**
   - In a medium saucepan, combine the chopped rhubarb, sugar, and water.
   - Cook over medium heat, stirring occasionally, until the rhubarb breaks down and becomes soft, about 10-15 minutes.
   - Remove from heat and let it cool slightly.
   - Transfer the cooked rhubarb to a blender or food processor and blend until smooth.
   - Let the rhubarb compote cool completely before using.
2. **Prepare the Custard Base:**
   - In a medium saucepan, combine the heavy cream, whole milk, and granulated sugar.
   - Heat the mixture over medium heat, stirring occasionally, until it begins to steam and tiny bubbles form around the edges. Do not let it boil.
   - In a separate bowl, whisk the egg yolks until they are pale and slightly thickened.
   - Gradually whisk about 1/2 cup of the warm cream mixture into the egg yolks to temper them.
   - Slowly pour the tempered egg yolk mixture back into the saucepan with the remaining cream mixture, stirring constantly.
   - Return the saucepan to medium-low heat. Cook the mixture, stirring constantly with a wooden spoon or heatproof spatula, until it thickens and

coats the back of the spoon. This should take about 5-7 minutes. Do not let it boil.
- Remove from heat and strain the custard through a fine-mesh sieve into a clean bowl to remove any cooked egg bits.
- Stir in the vanilla extract. Let the custard cool to room temperature, then cover and refrigerate for at least 4 hours or overnight until thoroughly chilled.

3. **Combine Rhubarb and Custard:**
    - Once the custard is chilled, pour it into your ice cream maker and churn according to the manufacturer's instructions. This usually takes about 20-25 minutes.
    - During the last few minutes of churning, add spoonfuls of the rhubarb compote into the ice cream, swirling gently with a spoon or spatula to create ribbons.

4. **Freeze the Ice Cream:**
    - Transfer the churned rhubarb and custard ice cream into a freezer-safe container, alternating layers of ice cream with more rhubarb compote swirls if desired.
    - Cover tightly with plastic wrap or a lid and freeze for at least 4 hours or until firm.

5. **Serve:**
    - Scoop and enjoy your homemade rhubarb and custard ice cream!

This recipe yields a creamy, tangy-sweet ice cream with vibrant swirls of rhubarb compote throughout. It's a delightful treat for any occasion, capturing the essence of rhubarb and custard in a frozen dessert form.

Lemon Curd Ice Cream

Ingredients:

For the Lemon Curd:

- 3-4 large lemons (to make about 1/2 cup (120 ml) lemon juice)
- Zest of 1 lemon
- 1 cup (200 g) granulated sugar
- 1/2 cup (115 g) unsalted butter, room temperature
- 4 large eggs

For the Ice Cream Base:

- 2 cups (480 ml) heavy cream
- 1 cup (240 ml) whole milk
- 3/4 cup (150 g) granulated sugar
- 5 large egg yolks
- 1 teaspoon vanilla extract

Instructions:

1. **Prepare the Lemon Curd:**
    - Zest one of the lemons and set the zest aside.
    - Juice enough lemons to obtain 1/2 cup (120 ml) of fresh lemon juice.
    - In a heatproof bowl set over a pot of simmering water (double boiler method), whisk together the lemon juice, lemon zest, sugar, butter, and eggs.
    - Cook the mixture, whisking constantly, until it thickens and coats the back of a spoon, about 10-15 minutes.
    - Remove from heat and strain through a fine-mesh sieve into a clean bowl to remove any bits of zest or cooked egg.
    - Let the lemon curd cool to room temperature, then cover and refrigerate until completely chilled, at least 4 hours or overnight.
2. **Prepare the Ice Cream Base:**
    - In a medium saucepan, combine the heavy cream, whole milk, and granulated sugar.
    - Heat the mixture over medium heat, stirring occasionally, until it begins to steam and tiny bubbles form around the edges. Do not let it boil.
    - In a separate bowl, whisk the egg yolks until they are pale and slightly thickened.

- Gradually whisk about 1/2 cup of the warm cream mixture into the egg yolks to temper them.
- Slowly pour the tempered egg yolk mixture back into the saucepan with the remaining cream mixture, stirring constantly.
- Return the saucepan to medium-low heat. Cook the mixture, stirring constantly with a wooden spoon or heatproof spatula, until it thickens and coats the back of the spoon. This should take about 5-7 minutes. Do not let it boil.
- Remove from heat and strain the custard through a fine-mesh sieve into a clean bowl to remove any cooked egg bits.
- Stir in the vanilla extract. Let the custard cool to room temperature, then cover and refrigerate for at least 4 hours or overnight until thoroughly chilled.

3. **Combine Lemon Curd and Ice Cream Base:**
   - Once the custard is chilled, whisk in the chilled lemon curd until well combined.
4. **Churn the Ice Cream:**
   - Pour the lemon custard mixture into your ice cream maker and churn according to the manufacturer's instructions. This usually takes about 20-25 minutes.
5. **Freeze the Ice Cream:**
   - Transfer the churned lemon curd ice cream into a freezer-safe container.
   - Cover tightly with plastic wrap or a lid and freeze for at least 4 hours or until firm.
6. **Serve:**
   - Scoop and enjoy your creamy and tangy homemade lemon curd ice cream!

This recipe yields a beautifully smooth and flavorful lemon curd ice cream, perfect for citrus lovers. The combination of creamy custard base and tangy lemon curd makes for a refreshing and delightful dessert.

Blackberry Ice Cream

Ingredients:

For the Blackberry Puree:

- 2 cups (about 300g) fresh blackberries
- 1/4 cup (50g) granulated sugar
- 1 tablespoon lemon juice

For the Ice Cream Base:

- 2 cups (480ml) heavy cream
- 1 cup (240ml) whole milk
- 3/4 cup (150g) granulated sugar
- 5 large egg yolks
- 1 teaspoon vanilla extract

Instructions:

1. **Prepare the Blackberry Puree:**
    - In a blender or food processor, combine the fresh blackberries, sugar, and lemon juice.
    - Blend until smooth.
    - Strain the blackberry puree through a fine-mesh sieve to remove seeds. You should have about 1 cup of strained puree. Set aside.
2. **Prepare the Ice Cream Base:**
    - In a medium saucepan, combine the heavy cream, whole milk, and granulated sugar.
    - Heat the mixture over medium heat, stirring occasionally, until it begins to steam and tiny bubbles form around the edges. Do not let it boil.
    - In a separate bowl, whisk the egg yolks until they are pale and slightly thickened.
    - Gradually whisk about 1/2 cup of the warm cream mixture into the egg yolks to temper them.
    - Slowly pour the tempered egg yolk mixture back into the saucepan with the remaining cream mixture, stirring constantly.
    - Return the saucepan to medium-low heat. Cook the mixture, stirring constantly with a wooden spoon or heatproof spatula, until it thickens and coats the back of the spoon. This should take about 5-7 minutes. Do not let it boil.

- Remove from heat and strain the custard through a fine-mesh sieve into a clean bowl to remove any cooked egg bits.
- Stir in the vanilla extract. Let the custard cool to room temperature, then cover and refrigerate for at least 4 hours or overnight until thoroughly chilled.

3. **Combine Blackberry Puree and Ice Cream Base:**
   - Once the custard is chilled, whisk in the blackberry puree until well combined.
4. **Churn the Ice Cream:**
   - Pour the blackberry custard mixture into your ice cream maker and churn according to the manufacturer's instructions. This usually takes about 20-25 minutes.
5. **Freeze the Ice Cream:**
   - Transfer the churned blackberry ice cream into a freezer-safe container.
   - Cover tightly with plastic wrap or a lid and freeze for at least 4 hours or until firm.
6. **Serve:**
   - Scoop and enjoy your creamy and fruity homemade blackberry ice cream!

This recipe results in a smooth and refreshing blackberry ice cream with vibrant fruit flavor. It's perfect for summer or anytime you crave a burst of berry goodness in a frozen treat.

Gingerbread Ice Cream

Ingredients:

For the Gingerbread Mix-ins:

- 1/2 cup (100g) granulated sugar
- 1/4 cup (60ml) water
- 2 tablespoons molasses
- 1 teaspoon ground ginger
- 1/2 teaspoon ground cinnamon
- 1/4 teaspoon ground cloves
- 1/4 teaspoon ground nutmeg
- Pinch of salt

For the Ice Cream Base:

- 2 cups (480ml) heavy cream
- 1 cup (240ml) whole milk
- 3/4 cup (150g) granulated sugar
- 5 large egg yolks
- 1 teaspoon vanilla extract

Instructions:

1. **Prepare the Gingerbread Mix-ins:**
    - In a small saucepan, combine the sugar, water, molasses, ground ginger, cinnamon, cloves, nutmeg, and salt.
    - Cook over medium heat, stirring constantly, until the sugar has dissolved and the mixture is well combined.
    - Remove from heat and let it cool completely.
2. **Prepare the Ice Cream Base:**
    - In a medium saucepan, combine the heavy cream, whole milk, and granulated sugar.
    - Heat the mixture over medium heat, stirring occasionally, until it begins to steam and tiny bubbles form around the edges. Do not let it boil.
    - In a separate bowl, whisk the egg yolks until they are pale and slightly thickened.
    - Gradually whisk about 1/2 cup of the warm cream mixture into the egg yolks to temper them.

- Slowly pour the tempered egg yolk mixture back into the saucepan with the remaining cream mixture, stirring constantly.
- Return the saucepan to medium-low heat. Cook the mixture, stirring constantly with a wooden spoon or heatproof spatula, until it thickens and coats the back of the spoon. This should take about 5-7 minutes. Do not let it boil.
- Remove from heat and strain the custard through a fine-mesh sieve into a clean bowl to remove any cooked egg bits.
- Stir in the vanilla extract. Let the custard cool to room temperature, then cover and refrigerate for at least 4 hours or overnight until thoroughly chilled.

3. **Combine Gingerbread Mix-ins and Ice Cream Base:**
   - Once the custard is chilled, stir in the cooled gingerbread mix-ins until evenly distributed.
4. **Churn the Ice Cream:**
   - Pour the gingerbread ice cream mixture into your ice cream maker and churn according to the manufacturer's instructions. This usually takes about 20-25 minutes.
5. **Freeze the Ice Cream:**
   - Transfer the churned gingerbread ice cream into a freezer-safe container.
   - Cover tightly with plastic wrap or a lid and freeze for at least 4 hours or until firm.
6. **Serve:**
   - Scoop and enjoy your creamy and spiced homemade gingerbread ice cream!

This recipe captures the warm and spicy flavors of gingerbread in a cool and creamy dessert. It's perfect for the holiday season or anytime you want to indulge in a festive treat.

Cherry Bakewell Ice Cream

Ingredients:

For the Cherry Compote:

- 2 cups (about 300g) fresh or frozen cherries, pitted
- 1/4 cup (50g) granulated sugar
- 1 tablespoon lemon juice
- 1/2 teaspoon almond extract

For the Almond Brittle:

- 1/2 cup (100g) granulated sugar
- 1/4 cup (60ml) water
- 1/2 cup (50g) sliced almonds

For the Ice Cream Base:

- 2 cups (480ml) heavy cream
- 1 cup (240ml) whole milk
- 3/4 cup (150g) granulated sugar
- 5 large egg yolks
- 1 teaspoon almond extract
- 1/2 cup (120g) cherry jam or preserves

Instructions:

1. **Prepare the Cherry Compote:**
    - In a medium saucepan, combine the cherries, sugar, lemon juice, and almond extract.
    - Cook over medium heat, stirring occasionally, until the cherries release their juices and the mixture thickens slightly, about 10-15 minutes.
    - Remove from heat and let it cool completely. Transfer to a container and refrigerate until ready to use.
2. **Prepare the Almond Brittle:**
    - Line a baking sheet with parchment paper or a silicone mat.
    - In a small saucepan, combine the sugar and water over medium-high heat.
    - Stir until the sugar dissolves, then let it boil without stirring until it reaches a light amber color, about 5-7 minutes.
    - Remove from heat and quickly stir in the sliced almonds.

- Immediately pour the mixture onto the prepared baking sheet, spreading it out into a thin, even layer.
- Let it cool completely, then break into small pieces. Set aside.

3. **Prepare the Ice Cream Base:**
    - In a medium saucepan, combine the heavy cream, whole milk, and granulated sugar.
    - Heat the mixture over medium heat, stirring occasionally, until it begins to steam and tiny bubbles form around the edges. Do not let it boil.
    - In a separate bowl, whisk the egg yolks until they are pale and slightly thickened.
    - Gradually whisk about 1/2 cup of the warm cream mixture into the egg yolks to temper them.
    - Slowly pour the tempered egg yolk mixture back into the saucepan with the remaining cream mixture, stirring constantly.
    - Return the saucepan to medium-low heat. Cook the mixture, stirring constantly with a wooden spoon or heatproof spatula, until it thickens and coats the back of the spoon. This should take about 5-7 minutes. Do not let it boil.
    - Remove from heat and strain the custard through a fine-mesh sieve into a clean bowl to remove any cooked egg bits.
    - Stir in the almond extract. Let the custard cool to room temperature, then cover and refrigerate for at least 4 hours or overnight until thoroughly chilled.

4. **Assemble the Ice Cream:**
    - Once the custard is chilled, stir in the cherry jam or preserves until well combined.

5. **Churn the Ice Cream:**
    - Pour the cherry almond ice cream mixture into your ice cream maker and churn according to the manufacturer's instructions. This usually takes about 20-25 minutes.

6. **Add Cherry Compote and Almond Brittle:**
    - During the last few minutes of churning, add spoonfuls of the chilled cherry compote and almond brittle pieces into the ice cream, swirling gently with a spoon or spatula to distribute evenly.

7. **Freeze the Ice Cream:**
    - Transfer the churned Cherry Bakewell ice cream into a freezer-safe container.
    - Cover tightly with plastic wrap or a lid and freeze for at least 4 hours or until firm.

8. **Serve:**
    - Scoop and enjoy your homemade Cherry Bakewell ice cream with delightful almond brittle and cherry swirls!

This recipe captures the essence of Cherry Bakewell in a creamy and indulgent ice cream form, perfect for any dessert occasion.

Marmalade Ice Cream

Ingredients:

- 1 cup (240ml) whole milk
- 1 cup (240ml) heavy cream
- 3/4 cup (150g) granulated sugar
- 4 large egg yolks
- 1/2 cup (120g) orange marmalade
- Zest of 1 orange
- 1 teaspoon vanilla extract
- Pinch of salt

Instructions:

1. **Prepare the Custard Base:**
    - In a medium saucepan, combine the whole milk, heavy cream, and half of the granulated sugar (about 1/2 cup). Heat over medium heat, stirring occasionally, until it begins to steam and small bubbles form around the edges. Do not let it boil.
    - In a separate bowl, whisk together the egg yolks and the remaining sugar until pale and slightly thickened.
    - Gradually pour the warm milk and cream mixture into the egg yolks, whisking constantly to temper the eggs.
    - Pour the tempered egg mixture back into the saucepan. Cook over medium-low heat, stirring constantly with a wooden spoon or spatula, until the mixture thickens enough to coat the back of the spoon and reaches around 170°F (77°C) on a thermometer. This will take about 5-7 minutes. Be careful not to let it boil.
    - Remove from heat and immediately strain the custard through a fine-mesh sieve into a clean bowl to remove any bits of cooked egg.
    - Stir in the vanilla extract, orange zest, and a pinch of salt. Let the custard cool to room temperature, then cover and refrigerate for at least 4 hours or overnight until thoroughly chilled.
2. **Churn the Ice Cream:**
    - Once the custard is chilled, whisk in the orange marmalade until well combined.
    - Pour the mixture into your ice cream maker and churn according to the manufacturer's instructions, usually about 20-25 minutes or until the ice cream reaches a soft-serve consistency.

3. **Freeze the Ice Cream:**
   - Transfer the churned Marmalade Ice Cream into a freezer-safe container.
   - Cover tightly with plastic wrap or a lid to prevent ice crystals from forming.
   - Freeze for at least 4 hours or until firm.
4. **Serve:**
   - Scoop and enjoy your creamy and tangy homemade Marmalade Ice Cream!

This recipe yields a smooth and flavorful ice cream with the distinct citrusy notes of orange marmalade, perfect for a refreshing dessert.

Peach Melba Ice Cream

Ingredients:

For the Peach Puree:

- 2 cups (about 3-4 medium) ripe peaches, peeled, pitted, and chopped
- 1/4 cup (50g) granulated sugar
- 1 tablespoon lemon juice

For the Raspberry Sauce:

- 1 cup (about 150g) fresh or frozen raspberries
- 2 tablespoons granulated sugar
- 1 tablespoon lemon juice

For the Ice Cream Base:

- 2 cups (480ml) heavy cream
- 1 cup (240ml) whole milk
- 3/4 cup (150g) granulated sugar
- 5 large egg yolks
- 1 teaspoon vanilla extract

Instructions:

1. **Prepare the Peach Puree:**
    - In a blender or food processor, combine the chopped peaches, sugar, and lemon juice.
    - Blend until smooth.
    - Strain the peach puree through a fine-mesh sieve to remove any chunks. Set aside.
2. **Prepare the Raspberry Sauce:**
    - In a small saucepan, combine the raspberries, sugar, and lemon juice.
    - Cook over medium heat, stirring occasionally, until the raspberries break down and the mixture thickens slightly, about 5-7 minutes.
    - Remove from heat and let it cool slightly.
    - Transfer the raspberry sauce to a blender or food processor and blend until smooth.
    - Strain the sauce through a fine-mesh sieve to remove the seeds. Set aside.
3. **Prepare the Ice Cream Base:**

- In a medium saucepan, combine the heavy cream, whole milk, and granulated sugar.
- Heat the mixture over medium heat, stirring occasionally, until it begins to steam and tiny bubbles form around the edges. Do not let it boil.
- In a separate bowl, whisk the egg yolks until they are pale and slightly thickened.
- Gradually whisk about 1/2 cup of the warm cream mixture into the egg yolks to temper them.
- Slowly pour the tempered egg yolk mixture back into the saucepan with the remaining cream mixture, stirring constantly.
- Return the saucepan to medium-low heat. Cook the mixture, stirring constantly with a wooden spoon or heatproof spatula, until it thickens and coats the back of the spoon. This should take about 5-7 minutes. Do not let it boil.
- Remove from heat and strain the custard through a fine-mesh sieve into a clean bowl to remove any cooked egg bits.
- Stir in the vanilla extract. Let the custard cool to room temperature, then cover and refrigerate for at least 4 hours or overnight until thoroughly chilled.

4. **Combine Peach Puree and Raspberry Sauce with Ice Cream Base:**
   - Once the custard is chilled, stir in the peach puree until well combined.

5. **Churn the Ice Cream:**
   - Pour the peach ice cream mixture into your ice cream maker and churn according to the manufacturer's instructions. This usually takes about 20-25 minutes.

6. **Add Raspberry Sauce Swirl:**
   - During the last few minutes of churning, drizzle in the raspberry sauce. Use a spoon or spatula to swirl the sauce into the ice cream, creating ribbons.

7. **Freeze the Ice Cream:**
   - Transfer the churned Peach Melba ice cream into a freezer-safe container.
   - Cover tightly with plastic wrap or a lid and freeze for at least 4 hours or until firm.

8. **Serve:**
   - Scoop and enjoy your creamy and fruity homemade Peach Melba Ice Cream!

This recipe captures the essence of the classic Peach Melba dessert in a refreshing and creamy ice cream form, perfect for enjoying the flavors of summer.

Blackcurrant Ice Cream

Ingredients:

For the Blackcurrant Puree:

- 2 cups (about 300g) fresh or frozen blackcurrants
- 1/2 cup (100g) granulated sugar
- 1 tablespoon lemon juice

For the Ice Cream Base:

- 2 cups (480ml) heavy cream
- 1 cup (240ml) whole milk
- 3/4 cup (150g) granulated sugar
- 5 large egg yolks
- 1 teaspoon vanilla extract

Instructions:

1. **Prepare the Blackcurrant Puree:**
    - In a medium saucepan, combine the blackcurrants, granulated sugar, and lemon juice.
    - Cook over medium heat, stirring occasionally, until the blackcurrants break down and release their juices, about 10-15 minutes.
    - Remove from heat and let the mixture cool slightly.
    - Transfer the cooked blackcurrants to a blender or food processor and blend until smooth.
    - Strain the puree through a fine-mesh sieve to remove any seeds. Set aside to cool completely.
2. **Prepare the Ice Cream Base:**
    - In a medium saucepan, combine the heavy cream, whole milk, and granulated sugar.
    - Heat the mixture over medium heat, stirring occasionally, until it begins to steam and small bubbles form around the edges. Do not let it boil.
    - In a separate bowl, whisk together the egg yolks until they are pale and slightly thickened.
    - Gradually whisk about 1/2 cup of the warm cream mixture into the egg yolks to temper them.
    - Slowly pour the tempered egg yolk mixture back into the saucepan with the remaining cream mixture, stirring constantly.

- Cook the mixture over medium-low heat, stirring constantly with a wooden spoon or heatproof spatula, until it thickens and coats the back of the spoon. This usually takes about 5-7 minutes. Do not let it boil.
- Remove from heat and strain the custard through a fine-mesh sieve into a clean bowl to remove any cooked egg bits.
- Stir in the vanilla extract. Let the custard cool to room temperature, then cover and refrigerate for at least 4 hours or overnight until thoroughly chilled.

3. **Combine Blackcurrant Puree with Ice Cream Base:**
   - Once the custard is chilled, stir in the cooled blackcurrant puree until well combined.
4. **Churn the Ice Cream:**
   - Pour the blackcurrant ice cream mixture into your ice cream maker and churn according to the manufacturer's instructions. This usually takes about 20-25 minutes, or until the ice cream reaches a soft-serve consistency.
5. **Freeze the Ice Cream:**
   - Transfer the churned blackcurrant ice cream into a freezer-safe container.
   - Cover tightly with plastic wrap or a lid and freeze for at least 4 hours or until firm.
6. **Serve:**
   - Scoop and enjoy your creamy and fruity homemade Blackcurrant Ice Cream!

This recipe yields a smooth and vibrant ice cream with the distinctive tartness of blackcurrants. It's perfect for summer or any time you crave a refreshing and unique frozen dessert.

Apple Crumble Ice Cream

Ingredients:

For the Apple Compote:

- 2 cups (about 2-3 medium) apples, peeled, cored, and diced (such as Granny Smith or any cooking apple)
- 2 tablespoons unsalted butter
- 1/4 cup (50g) brown sugar
- 1 teaspoon ground cinnamon
- 1/4 teaspoon ground nutmeg
- Pinch of salt

For the Crumble Mix-ins:

- 1/2 cup (60g) all-purpose flour
- 1/4 cup (50g) granulated sugar
- 1/4 cup (50g) brown sugar
- 1/2 teaspoon ground cinnamon
- Pinch of salt
- 1/4 cup (60g) cold unsalted butter, cut into small pieces

For the Ice Cream Base:

- 2 cups (480ml) heavy cream
- 1 cup (240ml) whole milk
- 3/4 cup (150g) granulated sugar
- 5 large egg yolks
- 1 teaspoon vanilla extract

Instructions:

1. **Prepare the Apple Compote:**
    - In a large skillet or saucepan, melt the butter over medium heat.
    - Add the diced apples, brown sugar, ground cinnamon, ground nutmeg, and a pinch of salt.
    - Cook, stirring occasionally, until the apples are softened and caramelized, about 8-10 minutes.
    - Remove from heat and let the apple compote cool completely. Transfer to a bowl and refrigerate until ready to use.

2. **Prepare the Crumble Mix-ins:**
   - Preheat your oven to 350°F (175°C).
   - In a medium bowl, combine the flour, granulated sugar, brown sugar, ground cinnamon, and a pinch of salt.
   - Add the cold butter pieces and use your fingers or a pastry cutter to blend the mixture until it resembles coarse crumbs.
   - Spread the crumble mixture evenly on a baking sheet lined with parchment paper.
   - Bake for about 10-12 minutes, or until golden brown and crispy.
   - Remove from the oven and let the crumble cool completely. Break it into small pieces. Set aside.
3. **Prepare the Ice Cream Base:**
   - In a medium saucepan, combine the heavy cream, whole milk, and granulated sugar.
   - Heat the mixture over medium heat, stirring occasionally, until it begins to steam and tiny bubbles form around the edges. Do not let it boil.
   - In a separate bowl, whisk together the egg yolks until they are pale and slightly thickened.
   - Gradually whisk about 1/2 cup of the warm cream mixture into the egg yolks to temper them.
   - Slowly pour the tempered egg yolk mixture back into the saucepan with the remaining cream mixture, stirring constantly.
   - Cook the mixture over medium-low heat, stirring constantly with a wooden spoon or heatproof spatula, until it thickens and coats the back of the spoon. This usually takes about 5-7 minutes. Do not let it boil.
   - Remove from heat and strain the custard through a fine-mesh sieve into a clean bowl to remove any cooked egg bits.
   - Stir in the vanilla extract. Let the custard cool to room temperature, then cover and refrigerate for at least 4 hours or overnight until thoroughly chilled.
4. **Assemble the Ice Cream:**
   - Once the custard is chilled, stir in the chilled apple compote and pieces of the cooled crumble until evenly distributed.
5. **Churn the Ice Cream:**
   - Pour the apple crumble ice cream mixture into your ice cream maker and churn according to the manufacturer's instructions. This usually takes about 20-25 minutes, or until the ice cream reaches a soft-serve consistency.
6. **Freeze the Ice Cream:**

- Transfer the churned Apple Crumble ice cream into a freezer-safe container.
- Cover tightly with plastic wrap or a lid and freeze for at least 4 hours or until firm.
7. **Serve:**
    - Scoop and enjoy your creamy and delicious homemade Apple Crumble Ice Cream!

This recipe captures the flavors of a classic apple crumble dessert in a delightful frozen form, perfect for enjoying any time of year.

Lavender and Honey Ice Cream

Ingredients:

- 2 cups (480ml) heavy cream
- 1 cup (240ml) whole milk
- 1/2 cup (120ml) honey
- 1/4 cup (50g) granulated sugar
- 2 tablespoons dried culinary lavender buds
- 5 large egg yolks
- 1 teaspoon vanilla extract

Instructions:

1. **Infuse the Cream Mixture:**
    - In a medium saucepan, combine the heavy cream, whole milk, honey, granulated sugar, and dried lavender buds.
    - Heat the mixture over medium heat, stirring occasionally, until it begins to steam and small bubbles form around the edges. Do not let it boil.
    - Once steaming, remove from heat, cover the saucepan, and let the mixture steep for about 20-30 minutes to infuse the lavender flavor. Stir occasionally to ensure the lavender distributes evenly.
2. **Strain the Mixture:**
    - After steeping, strain the cream mixture through a fine-mesh sieve into a clean bowl to remove the lavender buds. Press down on the lavender buds to extract as much flavor as possible. Discard the lavender buds.
3. **Prepare the Custard Base:**
    - In a separate bowl, whisk the egg yolks until they are pale and slightly thickened.
    - Gradually whisk about 1/2 cup of the lavender-infused cream mixture into the egg yolks to temper them.
    - Slowly pour the tempered egg yolk mixture back into the saucepan with the remaining lavender-infused cream mixture, stirring constantly.
4. **Cook the Custard:**
    - Cook the mixture over medium-low heat, stirring constantly with a wooden spoon or heatproof spatula, until it thickens and coats the back of the spoon. This usually takes about 5-7 minutes. Do not let it boil.
5. **Cool and Chill:**
    - Remove from heat and stir in the vanilla extract.

- Let the custard cool to room temperature, then cover and refrigerate for at least 4 hours or overnight until thoroughly chilled.
6. **Churn the Ice Cream:**
    - Once chilled, pour the lavender-infused custard into your ice cream maker and churn according to the manufacturer's instructions. This usually takes about 20-25 minutes, or until the ice cream reaches a soft-serve consistency.
7. **Freeze the Ice Cream:**
    - Transfer the churned Lavender and Honey Ice Cream into a freezer-safe container.
    - Cover tightly with plastic wrap or a lid and freeze for at least 4 hours or until firm.
8. **Serve:**
    - Scoop and enjoy your creamy and aromatic homemade Lavender and Honey Ice Cream!

This recipe captures the floral notes of lavender combined with the sweetness of honey in a beautifully creamy ice cream, perfect for a refreshing and unique dessert experience.

Spotted Dick Ice Cream

Ingredients:

For the Spotted Dick Mix-ins:

- 1/2 cup (100g) currants or raisins
- 1/4 cup (60ml) rum or orange juice (optional, for soaking)
- Zest of 1 lemon
- Zest of 1 orange

For the Ice Cream Base:

- 2 cups (480ml) heavy cream
- 1 cup (240ml) whole milk
- 3/4 cup (150g) granulated sugar
- 5 large egg yolks
- 1 teaspoon vanilla extract
- 1/2 teaspoon ground nutmeg
- 1/4 teaspoon ground cinnamon
- Pinch of salt

Instructions:

1. **Prepare the Spotted Dick Mix-ins:**
    - If using rum or orange juice, soak the currants or raisins in the liquid for about 30 minutes to plump them up. Drain before using.
    - In a small bowl, combine the currants or raisins with the lemon zest and orange zest. Set aside.
2. **Prepare the Ice Cream Base:**
    - In a medium saucepan, combine the heavy cream, whole milk, and granulated sugar.
    - Heat the mixture over medium heat, stirring occasionally, until it begins to steam and small bubbles form around the edges. Do not let it boil.
    - In a separate bowl, whisk together the egg yolks until they are pale and slightly thickened.
    - Gradually whisk about 1/2 cup of the warm cream mixture into the egg yolks to temper them.
    - Slowly pour the tempered egg yolk mixture back into the saucepan with the remaining cream mixture, stirring constantly.

- Cook the mixture over medium-low heat, stirring constantly with a wooden spoon or heatproof spatula, until it thickens and coats the back of the spoon. This usually takes about 5-7 minutes. Do not let it boil.
- Remove from heat and strain the custard through a fine-mesh sieve into a clean bowl to remove any cooked egg bits.
- Stir in the vanilla extract, ground nutmeg, ground cinnamon, and a pinch of salt. Let the custard cool to room temperature, then cover and refrigerate for at least 4 hours or overnight until thoroughly chilled.

3. **Combine Spotted Dick Mix-ins with Ice Cream Base:**
   - Once the custard is chilled, stir in the prepared Spotted Dick mix-ins until evenly distributed.
4. **Churn the Ice Cream:**
   - Pour the Spotted Dick ice cream mixture into your ice cream maker and churn according to the manufacturer's instructions. This usually takes about 20-25 minutes, or until the ice cream reaches a soft-serve consistency.
5. **Freeze the Ice Cream:**
   - Transfer the churned Spotted Dick ice cream into a freezer-safe container.
   - Cover tightly with plastic wrap or a lid and freeze for at least 4 hours or until firm.
6. **Serve:**
   - Scoop and enjoy your creamy and flavorful homemade Spotted Dick Ice Cream!

This recipe combines the rich flavors of currants (or raisins) with hints of citrus and warm spices in a creamy base, reminiscent of the beloved Spotted Dick pudding, transformed into a delightful frozen dessert.

Earl Grey Tea Ice Cream

Ingredients:

- 2 cups (480ml) heavy cream
- 1 cup (240ml) whole milk
- 3/4 cup (150g) granulated sugar
- 3 tablespoons loose Earl Grey tea leaves (or 3-4 tea bags)
- 5 large egg yolks
- 1 teaspoon vanilla extract

Instructions:

1. **Infuse the Cream Mixture:**
    - In a medium saucepan, combine the heavy cream, whole milk, granulated sugar, and Earl Grey tea leaves.
    - Heat the mixture over medium heat, stirring occasionally, until it begins to steam and small bubbles form around the edges. Do not let it boil.
    - Once steaming, remove from heat and cover the saucepan. Let the mixture steep for about 20-30 minutes to infuse the Earl Grey flavor. Stir occasionally to ensure the tea distributes evenly.
2. **Strain the Mixture:**
    - After steeping, strain the cream mixture through a fine-mesh sieve into a clean bowl to remove the tea leaves. Press down on the tea leaves to extract as much flavor as possible. Discard the tea leaves.
3. **Prepare the Custard Base:**
    - In a separate bowl, whisk the egg yolks until they are pale and slightly thickened.
    - Gradually whisk about 1/2 cup of the infused cream mixture into the egg yolks to temper them.
    - Slowly pour the tempered egg yolk mixture back into the saucepan with the remaining infused cream mixture, stirring constantly.
4. **Cook the Custard:**
    - Cook the mixture over medium-low heat, stirring constantly with a wooden spoon or heatproof spatula, until it thickens and coats the back of the spoon. This usually takes about 5-7 minutes. Do not let it boil.
5. **Cool and Chill:**
    - Remove from heat and stir in the vanilla extract.
    - Let the custard cool to room temperature, then cover and refrigerate for at least 4 hours or overnight until thoroughly chilled.

6. **Churn the Ice Cream:**
   - Once chilled, pour the Earl Grey-infused custard into your ice cream maker and churn according to the manufacturer's instructions. This usually takes about 20-25 minutes, or until the ice cream reaches a soft-serve consistency.
7. **Freeze the Ice Cream:**
   - Transfer the churned Earl Grey Tea Ice Cream into a freezer-safe container.
   - Cover tightly with plastic wrap or a lid and freeze for at least 4 hours or until firm.
8. **Serve:**
   - Scoop and enjoy your creamy and aromatic homemade Earl Grey Tea Ice Cream!

This recipe captures the floral and citrusy notes of Earl Grey tea in a smooth and creamy ice cream, perfect for tea lovers and dessert enthusiasts alike.

Pimm's Ice Cream

Ingredients:

- 1 cup (240ml) Pimm's No. 1
- 1 cup (240ml) heavy cream
- 1 cup (240ml) whole milk
- 3/4 cup (150g) granulated sugar
- 5 large egg yolks
- Zest of 1 lemon
- 1 teaspoon vanilla extract
- Pinch of salt

Instructions:

1. **Prepare the Custard Base:**
    - In a medium saucepan, combine the heavy cream, whole milk, Pimm's No. 1, granulated sugar, and lemon zest.
    - Heat the mixture over medium heat, stirring occasionally, until it begins to steam and small bubbles form around the edges. Do not let it boil.
    - In a separate bowl, whisk together the egg yolks until they are pale and slightly thickened.
    - Gradually whisk about 1/2 cup of the warm cream mixture into the egg yolks to temper them.
    - Slowly pour the tempered egg yolk mixture back into the saucepan with the remaining cream mixture, stirring constantly.
2. **Cook the Custard:**
    - Cook the mixture over medium-low heat, stirring constantly with a wooden spoon or heatproof spatula, until it thickens and coats the back of the spoon. This usually takes about 5-7 minutes. Do not let it boil.
3. **Cool and Chill:**
    - Remove from heat and stir in the vanilla extract and a pinch of salt.
    - Let the custard cool to room temperature, then cover and refrigerate for at least 4 hours or overnight until thoroughly chilled.
4. **Churn the Ice Cream:**
    - Once chilled, pour the Pimm's-infused custard into your ice cream maker and churn according to the manufacturer's instructions. This usually takes about 20-25 minutes, or until the ice cream reaches a soft-serve consistency.
5. **Freeze the Ice Cream:**

        - Transfer the churned Pimm's Ice Cream into a freezer-safe container.
        - Cover tightly with plastic wrap or a lid and freeze for at least 4 hours or until firm.
6. **Serve:**
        - Scoop and enjoy your creamy and refreshing homemade Pimm's Ice Cream!

This recipe captures the unique flavors of Pimm's No. 1 in a creamy and indulgent ice cream, perfect for enjoying on a warm day or as a delightful dessert after a summer meal.

Salted Caramel Ice Cream

Ingredients:

For the Salted Caramel Sauce:

- 1 cup (200g) granulated sugar
- 6 tablespoons unsalted butter, cut into pieces
- 1/2 cup (120ml) heavy cream
- 1 teaspoon sea salt (or to taste)

For the Ice Cream Base:

- 2 cups (480ml) heavy cream
- 1 cup (240ml) whole milk
- 3/4 cup (150g) granulated sugar
- 5 large egg yolks
- 1 teaspoon vanilla extract
- Additional sea salt, for sprinkling (optional)

Instructions:

1. **Prepare the Salted Caramel Sauce:**
    - Heat the granulated sugar in a heavy-bottomed saucepan over medium heat. Stir constantly with a heatproof spatula or wooden spoon as the sugar melts.
    - Once the sugar has melted completely and turned a deep amber color, add the butter pieces. Be careful as the mixture will bubble rapidly.
    - Stir the butter into the caramel until completely melted, about 2-3 minutes.
    - Slowly pour in the heavy cream while stirring constantly. Again, be cautious of bubbling.
    - Let the mixture boil for 1 minute, then remove from heat and stir in the sea salt.
    - Set aside to cool slightly while you prepare the ice cream base.
2. **Prepare the Ice Cream Base:**
    - In a medium saucepan, combine the heavy cream, whole milk, and granulated sugar.
    - Heat the mixture over medium heat, stirring occasionally, until it begins to steam and small bubbles form around the edges. Do not let it boil.
    - In a separate bowl, whisk together the egg yolks until they are pale and slightly thickened.

- Gradually whisk about 1/2 cup of the warm cream mixture into the egg yolks to temper them.
- Slowly pour the tempered egg yolk mixture back into the saucepan with the remaining cream mixture, stirring constantly.
- Cook the mixture over medium-low heat, stirring constantly with a wooden spoon or heatproof spatula, until it thickens and coats the back of the spoon. This usually takes about 5-7 minutes. Do not let it boil.
- Remove from heat and strain the custard through a fine-mesh sieve into a clean bowl to remove any cooked egg bits.
- Stir in the vanilla extract. Let the custard cool to room temperature, then cover and refrigerate for at least 4 hours or overnight until thoroughly chilled.

3. **Combine Salted Caramel Sauce with Ice Cream Base:**
    - Once the custard is chilled, stir in the prepared salted caramel sauce until well combined. You can swirl it in for a ripple effect or mix it completely for a caramel-infused ice cream.

4. **Churn the Ice Cream:**
    - Pour the salted caramel ice cream mixture into your ice cream maker and churn according to the manufacturer's instructions. This usually takes about 20-25 minutes, or until the ice cream reaches a soft-serve consistency.

5. **Freeze the Ice Cream:**
    - Transfer the churned Salted Caramel Ice Cream into a freezer-safe container.
    - Sprinkle with additional sea salt if desired.
    - Cover tightly with plastic wrap or a lid and freeze for at least 4 hours or until firm.

6. **Serve:**
    - Scoop and enjoy your creamy and indulgent homemade Salted Caramel Ice Cream!

This recipe yields a rich and velvety ice cream with the perfect balance of sweet caramel and a touch of sea salt, creating a delightful dessert that is sure to impress.

Irish Cream Liqueur Ice Cream

Ingredients:

- 1 cup (240ml) Irish cream liqueur (such as Baileys)
- 2 cups (480ml) heavy cream
- 1 cup (240ml) whole milk
- 3/4 cup (150g) granulated sugar
- 5 large egg yolks
- 1 teaspoon vanilla extract
- Chocolate shavings or cocoa powder, for garnish (optional)

Instructions:

1. **Prepare the Ice Cream Base:**
   - In a medium saucepan, combine the heavy cream, whole milk, Irish cream liqueur, and granulated sugar.
   - Heat the mixture over medium heat, stirring occasionally, until it begins to steam and small bubbles form around the edges. Do not let it boil.
   - In a separate bowl, whisk together the egg yolks until they are pale and slightly thickened.
   - Gradually whisk about 1/2 cup of the warm cream mixture into the egg yolks to temper them.
   - Slowly pour the tempered egg yolk mixture back into the saucepan with the remaining cream mixture, stirring constantly.
   - Cook the mixture over medium-low heat, stirring constantly with a wooden spoon or heatproof spatula, until it thickens and coats the back of the spoon. This usually takes about 5-7 minutes. Do not let it boil.
   - Remove from heat and strain the custard through a fine-mesh sieve into a clean bowl to remove any cooked egg bits.
   - Stir in the vanilla extract. Let the custard cool to room temperature, then cover and refrigerate for at least 4 hours or overnight until thoroughly chilled.
2. **Churn the Ice Cream:**
   - Once chilled, pour the Irish Cream Liqueur-infused custard into your ice cream maker and churn according to the manufacturer's instructions. This usually takes about 20-25 minutes, or until the ice cream reaches a soft-serve consistency.
3. **Freeze the Ice Cream:**

- Transfer the churned Irish Cream Liqueur Ice Cream into a freezer-safe container.
- Cover tightly with plastic wrap or a lid and freeze for at least 4 hours or until firm.
4. **Serve:**
    - Scoop and garnish with chocolate shavings or cocoa powder if desired.
    - Enjoy your creamy and decadent homemade Irish Cream Liqueur Ice Cream!

This recipe captures the smooth and luxurious flavors of Irish cream liqueur in a delightful frozen dessert, perfect for indulging in after a meal or as a special treat.

Whisky and Ginger Ice Cream

Ingredients:

- 1/2 cup (120ml) whisky (choose a whisky with a flavor profile you enjoy)
- 1/2 cup (120ml) heavy cream
- 1 cup (240ml) whole milk
- 3/4 cup (150g) granulated sugar
- 3-4 tablespoons finely chopped crystallized ginger
- 5 large egg yolks
- 1 teaspoon vanilla extract
- Pinch of salt

Instructions:

1. **Prepare the Ice Cream Base:**
    - In a medium saucepan, combine the heavy cream, whole milk, whisky, and granulated sugar.
    - Heat the mixture over medium heat, stirring occasionally, until it begins to steam and small bubbles form around the edges. Do not let it boil.
2. **Infuse with Ginger:**
    - Add the finely chopped crystallized ginger to the cream mixture and stir well.
    - Continue heating for another 5 minutes over medium-low heat, stirring occasionally, to infuse the ginger flavor into the mixture.
3. **Prepare the Custard:**
    - In a separate bowl, whisk together the egg yolks until they are pale and slightly thickened.
    - Gradually whisk about 1/2 cup of the warm cream mixture into the egg yolks to temper them.
    - Slowly pour the tempered egg yolk mixture back into the saucepan with the remaining cream mixture, stirring constantly.
    - Cook the mixture over medium-low heat, stirring constantly with a wooden spoon or heatproof spatula, until it thickens and coats the back of the spoon. This usually takes about 5-7 minutes. Do not let it boil.
    - Remove from heat and strain the custard through a fine-mesh sieve into a clean bowl to remove any cooked egg bits.
    - Stir in the vanilla extract and a pinch of salt. Let the custard cool to room temperature, then cover and refrigerate for at least 4 hours or overnight until thoroughly chilled.

4. **Churn the Ice Cream:**
   - Once chilled, pour the Whisky and Ginger-infused custard into your ice cream maker and churn according to the manufacturer's instructions. This usually takes about 20-25 minutes, or until the ice cream reaches a soft-serve consistency.
5. **Freeze the Ice Cream:**
   - Transfer the churned Whisky and Ginger Ice Cream into a freezer-safe container.
   - Cover tightly with plastic wrap or a lid and freeze for at least 4 hours or until firm.
6. **Serve:**
   - Scoop and enjoy your creamy and flavorful homemade Whisky and Ginger Ice Cream!

This recipe combines the robust flavor of whisky with the spicy warmth of ginger, creating a sophisticated and delightful frozen dessert that's perfect for special occasions or as a unique treat any time of year. Adjust the amount of whisky and ginger to suit your taste preferences for a personalized touch.

Gooseberry Ice Cream

Ingredients:

- 2 cups (480ml) heavy cream
- 1 cup (240ml) whole milk
- 3/4 cup (150g) granulated sugar
- 2 cups fresh or frozen gooseberries, washed and stems removed
- 5 large egg yolks
- 1 teaspoon vanilla extract
- Pinch of salt

Instructions:

1. **Prepare the Gooseberries:**
    - In a medium saucepan, combine the gooseberries with 1/4 cup of sugar. Cook over medium heat, stirring occasionally, until the gooseberries soften and release their juices. This takes about 8-10 minutes.
    - Remove from heat and let the gooseberries cool slightly. Blend or mash them into a puree using a blender or food processor. Set aside.
2. **Prepare the Ice Cream Base:**
    - In a medium saucepan, combine the heavy cream, whole milk, and remaining 1/2 cup of sugar.
    - Heat the mixture over medium heat, stirring occasionally, until it begins to steam and small bubbles form around the edges. Do not let it boil.
3. **Combine Gooseberry Puree with Ice Cream Base:**
    - Once steaming, remove from heat and stir in the gooseberry puree. Mix well until thoroughly combined.
4. **Prepare the Custard:**
    - In a separate bowl, whisk together the egg yolks until they are pale and slightly thickened.
    - Gradually whisk about 1/2 cup of the warm cream mixture into the egg yolks to temper them.
    - Slowly pour the tempered egg yolk mixture back into the saucepan with the remaining cream mixture, stirring constantly.
5. **Cook the Custard:**
    - Cook the mixture over medium-low heat, stirring constantly with a wooden spoon or heatproof spatula, until it thickens and coats the back of the spoon. This usually takes about 5-7 minutes. Do not let it boil.
6. **Cool and Chill:**

- Remove from heat and strain the custard through a fine-mesh sieve into a clean bowl to remove any cooked egg bits.
- Stir in the vanilla extract and a pinch of salt. Let the custard cool to room temperature, then cover and refrigerate for at least 4 hours or overnight until thoroughly chilled.

7. **Churn the Ice Cream:**
   - Once chilled, pour the Gooseberry-infused custard into your ice cream maker and churn according to the manufacturer's instructions. This usually takes about 20-25 minutes, or until the ice cream reaches a soft-serve consistency.

8. **Freeze the Ice Cream:**
   - Transfer the churned Gooseberry Ice Cream into a freezer-safe container.
   - Cover tightly with plastic wrap or a lid and freeze for at least 4 hours or until firm.

9. **Serve:**
   - Scoop and enjoy your creamy and fruity homemade Gooseberry Ice Cream!

This recipe captures the unique tartness and sweetness of gooseberries in a smooth and creamy ice cream, perfect for a refreshing and delightful dessert experience. Adjust the sugar quantity based on the tartness of your gooseberries and enjoy this seasonal treat!

Mulled Wine Ice Cream

Ingredients:

- 2 cups (480ml) heavy cream
- 1 cup (240ml) whole milk
- 3/4 cup (150g) granulated sugar
- 1 cup mulled red wine (see instructions below for mulled wine preparation)
- Zest of 1 orange
- Zest of 1 lemon
- 5 large egg yolks
- 1 teaspoon vanilla extract
- 1/2 teaspoon ground cinnamon
- 1/4 teaspoon ground cloves
- Pinch of salt

Instructions:

1. **Prepare the Mulled Wine:**
    - To make mulled wine, combine 1 bottle (750ml) of red wine with 1/4 cup of honey or sugar, 1 cinnamon stick, 4-6 cloves, 1 star anise, and zest of 1 orange and 1 lemon in a saucepan.
    - Heat over medium-low heat, stirring occasionally, until the mixture begins to steam and the flavors meld together. Do not boil.
    - Once steaming, reduce heat to low and let simmer for about 15-20 minutes to infuse the flavors. Remove from heat and let cool. Strain to remove the spices and zest, leaving you with 1 cup of mulled wine for the ice cream.
2. **Prepare the Ice Cream Base:**
    - In a medium saucepan, combine the heavy cream, whole milk, and granulated sugar.
    - Heat the mixture over medium heat, stirring occasionally, until it begins to steam and small bubbles form around the edges. Do not let it boil.
3. **Combine Mulled Wine with Ice Cream Base:**
    - Stir in 1 cup of mulled wine, orange zest, and lemon zest into the warm cream mixture. Mix well.
4. **Prepare the Custard:**
    - In a separate bowl, whisk together the egg yolks until they are pale and slightly thickened.

- Gradually whisk about 1/2 cup of the warm cream mixture into the egg yolks to temper them.
- Slowly pour the tempered egg yolk mixture back into the saucepan with the remaining cream mixture, stirring constantly.

5. **Cook the Custard:**
   - Cook the mixture over medium-low heat, stirring constantly with a wooden spoon or heatproof spatula, until it thickens and coats the back of the spoon. This usually takes about 5-7 minutes. Do not let it boil.

6. **Cool and Chill:**
   - Remove from heat and strain the custard through a fine-mesh sieve into a clean bowl to remove any cooked egg bits.
   - Stir in the vanilla extract, ground cinnamon, ground cloves, and a pinch of salt. Let the custard cool to room temperature, then cover and refrigerate for at least 4 hours or overnight until thoroughly chilled.

7. **Churn the Ice Cream:**
   - Once chilled, pour the Mulled Wine-infused custard into your ice cream maker and churn according to the manufacturer's instructions. This usually takes about 20-25 minutes, or until the ice cream reaches a soft-serve consistency.

8. **Freeze the Ice Cream:**
   - Transfer the churned Mulled Wine Ice Cream into a freezer-safe container.
   - Cover tightly with plastic wrap or a lid and freeze for at least 4 hours or until firm.

9. **Serve:**
   - Scoop and enjoy your creamy and spiced homemade Mulled Wine Ice Cream!

This recipe captures the cozy and aromatic flavors of mulled wine in a decadent frozen dessert, perfect for the holidays or any special occasion. Adjust the spices and sweetness to your taste preference for a personalized touch.

Lemon and Elderflower Ice Cream

Ingredients:

- 2 cups (480ml) heavy cream
- 1 cup (240ml) whole milk
- 3/4 cup (150g) granulated sugar
- Zest of 2 lemons
- 1/2 cup fresh lemon juice (from about 4-5 lemons)
- 1/4 cup elderflower cordial
- 5 large egg yolks
- 1 teaspoon vanilla extract
- Pinch of salt

Instructions:

1. **Prepare the Ice Cream Base:**
   - In a medium saucepan, combine the heavy cream, whole milk, granulated sugar, and lemon zest.
   - Heat the mixture over medium heat, stirring occasionally, until it begins to steam and small bubbles form around the edges. Do not let it boil.
2. **Add Lemon and Elderflower:**
   - Stir in the fresh lemon juice and elderflower cordial into the warm cream mixture. Mix well.
3. **Prepare the Custard:**
   - In a separate bowl, whisk together the egg yolks until they are pale and slightly thickened.
   - Gradually whisk about 1/2 cup of the warm cream mixture into the egg yolks to temper them.
   - Slowly pour the tempered egg yolk mixture back into the saucepan with the remaining cream mixture, stirring constantly.
4. **Cook the Custard:**
   - Cook the mixture over medium-low heat, stirring constantly with a wooden spoon or heatproof spatula, until it thickens and coats the back of the spoon. This usually takes about 5-7 minutes. Do not let it boil.
5. **Cool and Chill:**
   - Remove from heat and strain the custard through a fine-mesh sieve into a clean bowl to remove any cooked egg bits.

- Stir in the vanilla extract and a pinch of salt. Let the custard cool to room temperature, then cover and refrigerate for at least 4 hours or overnight until thoroughly chilled.
6. **Churn the Ice Cream:**
    - Once chilled, pour the Lemon and Elderflower-infused custard into your ice cream maker and churn according to the manufacturer's instructions. This usually takes about 20-25 minutes, or until the ice cream reaches a soft-serve consistency.
7. **Freeze the Ice Cream:**
    - Transfer the churned Lemon and Elderflower Ice Cream into a freezer-safe container.
    - Cover tightly with plastic wrap or a lid and freeze for at least 4 hours or until firm.
8. **Serve:**
    - Scoop and enjoy your creamy and refreshing homemade Lemon and Elderflower Ice Cream!

This recipe captures the vibrant citrus and floral flavors of lemon and elderflower in a delightful frozen dessert, perfect for enjoying on a sunny day or as a light and elegant finish to a meal. Adjust the sweetness and lemon intensity to suit your taste preferences for a personalized touch.

Cranachan Ice Cream

Ingredients:

- 2 cups (480ml) heavy cream
- 1 cup (240ml) whole milk
- 3/4 cup (150g) granulated sugar
- 1/4 cup whisky (optional)
- 1 cup fresh raspberries, plus extra for garnish
- 1/2 cup toasted oats (rolled oats, toasted until golden)
- Zest of 1 lemon
- 5 large egg yolks
- 1 teaspoon vanilla extract
- Pinch of salt

Instructions:

1. **Prepare the Ice Cream Base:**
   - In a medium saucepan, combine the heavy cream, whole milk, granulated sugar, and whisky (if using).
   - Heat the mixture over medium heat, stirring occasionally, until it begins to steam and small bubbles form around the edges. Do not let it boil.
2. **Prepare the Raspberries:**
   - In a small bowl, mash the raspberries with a fork until slightly chunky. Set aside.
3. **Toast the Oats:**
   - Heat a dry skillet over medium heat. Add the rolled oats and toast, stirring frequently, until golden brown and fragrant, about 5-7 minutes. Remove from heat and let cool.
4. **Prepare the Custard:**
   - In a separate bowl, whisk together the egg yolks until they are pale and slightly thickened.
   - Gradually whisk about 1/2 cup of the warm cream mixture into the egg yolks to temper them.
   - Slowly pour the tempered egg yolk mixture back into the saucepan with the remaining cream mixture, stirring constantly.
5. **Cook the Custard:**
   - Cook the mixture over medium-low heat, stirring constantly with a wooden spoon or heatproof spatula, until it thickens and coats the back of the spoon. This usually takes about 5-7 minutes. Do not let it boil.

6. **Cool and Chill:**
   - Remove from heat and strain the custard through a fine-mesh sieve into a clean bowl to remove any cooked egg bits.
   - Stir in the vanilla extract, lemon zest, and a pinch of salt. Let the custard cool to room temperature, then cover and refrigerate for at least 4 hours or overnight until thoroughly chilled.
7. **Churn the Ice Cream:**
   - Once chilled, pour the Cranachan-infused custard into your ice cream maker and churn according to the manufacturer's instructions. This usually takes about 20-25 minutes, or until the ice cream reaches a soft-serve consistency.
8. **Fold in Raspberries and Oats:**
   - During the last few minutes of churning, add the mashed raspberries and toasted oats to the ice cream maker. Let it mix until evenly distributed.
9. **Freeze the Ice Cream:**
   - Transfer the churned Cranachan Ice Cream into a freezer-safe container.
   - Cover tightly with plastic wrap or a lid and freeze for at least 4 hours or until firm.
10. **Serve:**
    - Scoop the Cranachan Ice Cream into bowls or cones.
    - Garnish with fresh raspberries and additional toasted oats if desired.
    - Enjoy your creamy and flavorful homemade Cranachan Ice Cream!

This recipe combines the traditional flavors of Cranachan into a creamy and delightful frozen dessert, perfect for celebrating Scottish cuisine or enjoying a unique twist on a classic dessert. Adjust the whisky and sweetness levels to suit your taste preferences.

Pumpkin Spice Ice Cream

Ingredients:

- 1 cup (240ml) pumpkin puree (canned or homemade)
- 1 teaspoon ground cinnamon
- 1/2 teaspoon ground ginger
- 1/4 teaspoon ground nutmeg
- 1/4 teaspoon ground cloves
- 2 cups (480ml) heavy cream
- 1 cup (240ml) whole milk
- 3/4 cup (150g) granulated sugar
- 5 large egg yolks
- 1 teaspoon vanilla extract
- Pinch of salt

Instructions:

1. **Prepare the Ice Cream Base:**
    - In a medium saucepan, combine the heavy cream, whole milk, pumpkin puree, ground cinnamon, ground ginger, ground nutmeg, and ground cloves.
    - Heat the mixture over medium heat, stirring occasionally, until it begins to steam and small bubbles form around the edges. Do not let it boil.
2. **Prepare the Custard:**
    - In a separate bowl, whisk together the egg yolks until they are pale and slightly thickened.
    - Gradually whisk about 1/2 cup of the warm cream mixture into the egg yolks to temper them.
    - Slowly pour the tempered egg yolk mixture back into the saucepan with the remaining cream mixture, stirring constantly.
3. **Cook the Custard:**
    - Cook the mixture over medium-low heat, stirring constantly with a wooden spoon or heatproof spatula, until it thickens and coats the back of the spoon. This usually takes about 5-7 minutes. Do not let it boil.
4. **Cool and Chill:**
    - Remove from heat and strain the custard through a fine-mesh sieve into a clean bowl to remove any cooked egg bits.

- Stir in the vanilla extract and a pinch of salt. Let the custard cool to room temperature, then cover and refrigerate for at least 4 hours or overnight until thoroughly chilled.
5. **Churn the Ice Cream:**
    - Once chilled, pour the Pumpkin Spice-infused custard into your ice cream maker and churn according to the manufacturer's instructions. This usually takes about 20-25 minutes, or until the ice cream reaches a soft-serve consistency.
6. **Freeze the Ice Cream:**
    - Transfer the churned Pumpkin Spice Ice Cream into a freezer-safe container.
    - Cover tightly with plastic wrap or a lid and freeze for at least 4 hours or until firm.
7. **Serve:**
    - Scoop and enjoy your creamy and flavorful homemade Pumpkin Spice Ice Cream!

This recipe captures the essence of fall with the warm spices and comforting flavor of pumpkin, making it a perfect treat for autumn or anytime you crave a taste of seasonal goodness. Adjust the spice levels according to your preference for a more intense or subtle flavor profile.

Treacle Tart Ice Cream

Ingredients:

- 1 cup (240ml) heavy cream
- 1 cup (240ml) whole milk
- 1/2 cup (120ml) golden syrup (treacle)
- Zest of 1 lemon
- 3/4 cup (150g) granulated sugar
- 5 large egg yolks
- 1 teaspoon vanilla extract
- Pinch of salt

Instructions:

1. **Prepare the Ice Cream Base:**
   - In a medium saucepan, combine the heavy cream, whole milk, golden syrup (treacle), and lemon zest.
   - Heat the mixture over medium heat, stirring occasionally, until it begins to steam and small bubbles form around the edges. Do not let it boil.
2. **Prepare the Custard:**
   - In a separate bowl, whisk together the egg yolks until they are pale and slightly thickened.
   - Gradually whisk about 1/2 cup of the warm cream mixture into the egg yolks to temper them.
   - Slowly pour the tempered egg yolk mixture back into the saucepan with the remaining cream mixture, stirring constantly.
3. **Cook the Custard:**
   - Cook the mixture over medium-low heat, stirring constantly with a wooden spoon or heatproof spatula, until it thickens and coats the back of the spoon. This usually takes about 5-7 minutes. Do not let it boil.
4. **Cool and Chill:**
   - Remove from heat and strain the custard through a fine-mesh sieve into a clean bowl to remove any cooked egg bits.
   - Stir in the vanilla extract and a pinch of salt. Let the custard cool to room temperature, then cover and refrigerate for at least 4 hours or overnight until thoroughly chilled.
5. **Churn the Ice Cream:**
   - Once chilled, pour the Treacle Tart-infused custard into your ice cream maker and churn according to the manufacturer's instructions. This

usually takes about 20-25 minutes, or until the ice cream reaches a soft-serve consistency.

6. **Freeze the Ice Cream:**
   - Transfer the churned Treacle Tart Ice Cream into a freezer-safe container.
   - Cover tightly with plastic wrap or a lid and freeze for at least 4 hours or until firm.
7. **Serve:**
   - Scoop and enjoy your creamy and indulgent homemade Treacle Tart Ice Cream!

This recipe captures the sweet, caramel-like flavor of treacle combined with the bright zestiness of lemon in a luxurious frozen dessert. It's a perfect treat for those who enjoy classic British flavors or want to experience a unique twist on traditional desserts. Adjust the sweetness level by varying the amount of golden syrup according to your taste preferences.

Coffee and Walnut Ice Cream

Ingredients:

- 2 cups (480ml) heavy cream
- 1 cup (240ml) whole milk
- 3/4 cup (150g) granulated sugar
- 3 tablespoons instant coffee granules
- 1 cup chopped walnuts, toasted
- 5 large egg yolks
- 1 teaspoon vanilla extract
- Pinch of salt

Instructions:

1. **Prepare the Ice Cream Base:**
    - In a medium saucepan, combine the heavy cream, whole milk, granulated sugar, and instant coffee granules.
    - Heat the mixture over medium heat, stirring occasionally, until it begins to steam and small bubbles form around the edges. Do not let it boil.
2. **Toast the Walnuts:**
    - While the cream mixture is heating, toast the chopped walnuts in a dry skillet over medium heat for about 5-7 minutes, or until they are lightly browned and fragrant. Stir frequently to prevent burning. Remove from heat and set aside.
3. **Prepare the Custard:**
    - In a separate bowl, whisk together the egg yolks until they are pale and slightly thickened.
    - Gradually whisk about 1/2 cup of the warm cream mixture into the egg yolks to temper them.
    - Slowly pour the tempered egg yolk mixture back into the saucepan with the remaining cream mixture, stirring constantly.
4. **Cook the Custard:**
    - Cook the mixture over medium-low heat, stirring constantly with a wooden spoon or heatproof spatula, until it thickens and coats the back of the spoon. This usually takes about 5-7 minutes. Do not let it boil.
5. **Cool and Chill:**
    - Remove from heat and strain the custard through a fine-mesh sieve into a clean bowl to remove any cooked egg bits.

- Stir in the vanilla extract and a pinch of salt. Let the custard cool to room temperature, then cover and refrigerate for at least 4 hours or overnight until thoroughly chilled.

6. **Churn the Ice Cream:**
   - Once chilled, pour the Coffee and Walnut-infused custard into your ice cream maker and churn according to the manufacturer's instructions. This usually takes about 20-25 minutes, or until the ice cream reaches a soft-serve consistency.

7. **Fold in Toasted Walnuts:**
   - During the last few minutes of churning, add the toasted walnuts to the ice cream maker. Let it mix until evenly distributed.

8. **Freeze the Ice Cream:**
   - Transfer the churned Coffee and Walnut Ice Cream into a freezer-safe container.
   - Cover tightly with plastic wrap or a lid and freeze for at least 4 hours or until firm.

9. **Serve:**
   - Scoop and enjoy your creamy and flavorful homemade Coffee and Walnut Ice Cream!

This recipe captures the bold flavor of coffee and the crunchy texture of toasted walnuts in a decadent frozen dessert. It's perfect for coffee lovers and those who enjoy a bit of nuttiness in their ice cream. Adjust the intensity of coffee flavor and sweetness according to your preference for a personalized treat.

Turkish Delight Ice Cream

Ingredients:

- 2 cups (480ml) heavy cream
- 1 cup (240ml) whole milk
- 3/4 cup (150g) granulated sugar
- 1/4 cup rosewater
- 1/2 cup Turkish delight (chopped into small pieces)
- 1/2 cup pistachios (chopped)
- 5 large egg yolks
- 1 teaspoon vanilla extract
- Pinch of salt
- Pink food coloring (optional)

Instructions:

1. **Prepare the Ice Cream Base:**
    - In a medium saucepan, combine the heavy cream, whole milk, granulated sugar, and rosewater.
    - Heat the mixture over medium heat, stirring occasionally, until it begins to steam and small bubbles form around the edges. Do not let it boil.
2. **Prepare the Turkish Delight and Pistachios:**
    - While the cream mixture is heating, chop the Turkish delight into small pieces and chop the pistachios.
3. **Prepare the Custard:**
    - In a separate bowl, whisk together the egg yolks until they are pale and slightly thickened.
    - Gradually whisk about 1/2 cup of the warm cream mixture into the egg yolks to temper them.
    - Slowly pour the tempered egg yolk mixture back into the saucepan with the remaining cream mixture, stirring constantly.
4. **Cook the Custard:**
    - Cook the mixture over medium-low heat, stirring constantly with a wooden spoon or heatproof spatula, until it thickens and coats the back of the spoon. This usually takes about 5-7 minutes. Do not let it boil.
5. **Cool and Chill:**
    - Remove from heat and strain the custard through a fine-mesh sieve into a clean bowl to remove any cooked egg bits.

- Stir in the vanilla extract and a pinch of salt. Optionally, add a few drops of pink food coloring for a light pink hue.
- Let the custard cool to room temperature, then cover and refrigerate for at least 4 hours or overnight until thoroughly chilled.

6. **Churn the Ice Cream:**
   - Once chilled, pour the Turkish Delight-infused custard into your ice cream maker and churn according to the manufacturer's instructions. This usually takes about 20-25 minutes, or until the ice cream reaches a soft-serve consistency.
7. **Fold in Turkish Delight and Pistachios:**
   - During the last few minutes of churning, add the chopped Turkish delight and pistachios to the ice cream maker. Let it mix until evenly distributed.
8. **Freeze the Ice Cream:**
   - Transfer the churned Turkish Delight Ice Cream into a freezer-safe container.
   - Cover tightly with plastic wrap or a lid and freeze for at least 4 hours or until firm.
9. **Serve:**
   - Scoop and enjoy your creamy and exotic homemade Turkish Delight Ice Cream!

This recipe captures the unique flavors of Turkish delight and pistachios in a delightful frozen dessert, perfect for indulging in a taste of the Middle East. Adjust the amount of rosewater and sweetness according to your preference for a personalized treat.

Matcha Green Tea Ice Cream

Ingredients:

- 2 cups (480ml) heavy cream
- 1 cup (240ml) whole milk
- 3/4 cup (150g) granulated sugar
- 3 tablespoons matcha green tea powder
- 5 large egg yolks
- 1 teaspoon vanilla extract
- Pinch of salt

Instructions:

1. **Prepare the Ice Cream Base:**
    - In a medium saucepan, combine the heavy cream, whole milk, granulated sugar, and matcha green tea powder.
    - Whisk together until the matcha powder is fully dissolved and the mixture is smooth.
    - Heat the mixture over medium heat, stirring occasionally, until it begins to steam and small bubbles form around the edges. Do not let it boil.
2. **Prepare the Custard:**
    - In a separate bowl, whisk together the egg yolks until they are pale and slightly thickened.
    - Gradually whisk about 1/2 cup of the warm matcha cream mixture into the egg yolks to temper them.
    - Slowly pour the tempered egg yolk mixture back into the saucepan with the remaining matcha cream mixture, stirring constantly.
3. **Cook the Custard:**
    - Cook the mixture over medium-low heat, stirring constantly with a wooden spoon or heatproof spatula, until it thickens and coats the back of the spoon. This usually takes about 5-7 minutes. Do not let it boil.
4. **Cool and Chill:**
    - Remove from heat and strain the custard through a fine-mesh sieve into a clean bowl to remove any cooked egg bits.
    - Stir in the vanilla extract and a pinch of salt. Let the custard cool to room temperature, then cover and refrigerate for at least 4 hours or overnight until thoroughly chilled.
5. **Churn the Ice Cream:**

- Once chilled, pour the Matcha Green Tea-infused custard into your ice cream maker and churn according to the manufacturer's instructions. This usually takes about 20-25 minutes, or until the ice cream reaches a soft-serve consistency.

6. **Freeze the Ice Cream:**
   - Transfer the churned Matcha Green Tea Ice Cream into a freezer-safe container.
   - Cover tightly with plastic wrap or a lid and freeze for at least 4 hours or until firm.
7. **Serve:**
   - Scoop and enjoy your creamy and vibrant homemade Matcha Green Tea Ice Cream!

This recipe captures the natural and slightly bitter-sweet flavor of matcha green tea in a smooth and creamy dessert. Adjust the amount of matcha powder and sweetness according to your taste preferences for a personalized treat.

Cardamom and Saffron Ice Cream

Ingredients:

- 2 cups (480ml) heavy cream
- 1 cup (240ml) whole milk
- 3/4 cup (150g) granulated sugar
- 1 teaspoon ground cardamom
- 1/4 teaspoon saffron threads
- 5 large egg yolks
- 1 teaspoon vanilla extract
- Pinch of salt

Instructions:

1. **Prepare the Saffron Infusion:**
    - In a small bowl, crush the saffron threads slightly with your fingers. Add 1-2 tablespoons of warm milk (from the 1 cup) to the saffron threads and let it steep for about 10-15 minutes to release the flavor and color.
2. **Prepare the Ice Cream Base:**
    - In a medium saucepan, combine the heavy cream, remaining whole milk, granulated sugar, and ground cardamom.
    - Heat the mixture over medium heat, stirring occasionally, until it begins to steam and small bubbles form around the edges. Do not let it boil.
3. **Prepare the Custard:**
    - In a separate bowl, whisk together the egg yolks until they are pale and slightly thickened.
    - Gradually whisk about 1/2 cup of the warm cream mixture into the egg yolks to temper them.
    - Slowly pour the tempered egg yolk mixture back into the saucepan with the remaining cream mixture, stirring constantly.
4. **Cook the Custard:**
    - Cook the mixture over medium-low heat, stirring constantly with a wooden spoon or heatproof spatula, until it thickens and coats the back of the spoon. This usually takes about 5-7 minutes. Do not let it boil.
5. **Incorporate Saffron and Chill:**
    - Remove from heat and strain the custard through a fine-mesh sieve into a clean bowl to remove any cooked egg bits.
    - Stir in the vanilla extract, the saffron infusion (including the threads), and a pinch of salt. Mix well.

- Let the custard cool to room temperature, then cover and refrigerate for at least 4 hours or overnight until thoroughly chilled.
6. **Churn the Ice Cream:**
    - Once chilled, pour the Cardamom and Saffron-infused custard into your ice cream maker and churn according to the manufacturer's instructions. This usually takes about 20-25 minutes, or until the ice cream reaches a soft-serve consistency.
7. **Freeze the Ice Cream:**
    - Transfer the churned Cardamom and Saffron Ice Cream into a freezer-safe container.
    - Cover tightly with plastic wrap or a lid and freeze for at least 4 hours or until firm.
8. **Serve:**
    - Scoop and enjoy your creamy and aromatic homemade Cardamom and Saffron Ice Cream!

This recipe captures the exotic flavors of cardamom and saffron in a smooth and luxurious frozen dessert, perfect for a special occasion or to indulge in a unique flavor experience. Adjust the amount of cardamom and saffron according to your taste preferences for a personalized touch.

Cucumber and Mint Ice Cream

Ingredients:

- 1 cup (240ml) heavy cream
- 1 cup (240ml) whole milk
- 3/4 cup (150g) granulated sugar
- 1 cup cucumber, peeled, seeded, and grated
- 1/2 cup fresh mint leaves, chopped
- 5 large egg yolks
- 1 teaspoon vanilla extract
- Pinch of salt
- Green food coloring (optional)

Instructions:

1. **Prepare the Cucumber and Mint Mixture:**
    - In a blender or food processor, puree the grated cucumber and chopped mint leaves until smooth. Set aside.
2. **Prepare the Ice Cream Base:**
    - In a medium saucepan, combine the heavy cream, whole milk, and granulated sugar over medium heat, stirring occasionally, until it begins to steam and small bubbles form around the edges. Do not let it boil.
3. **Prepare the Custard:**
    - In a separate bowl, whisk together the egg yolks until they are pale and slightly thickened.
    - Gradually whisk about 1/2 cup of the warm cream mixture into the egg yolks to temper them.
    - Slowly pour the tempered egg yolk mixture back into the saucepan with the remaining cream mixture, stirring constantly.
4. **Cook the Custard:**
    - Cook the mixture over medium-low heat, stirring constantly with a wooden spoon or heatproof spatula, until it thickens and coats the back of the spoon. This usually takes about 5-7 minutes. Do not let it boil.
5. **Incorporate Cucumber and Mint:**
    - Remove from heat and strain the custard through a fine-mesh sieve into a clean bowl to remove any cooked egg bits.
    - Stir in the cucumber and mint puree, vanilla extract, and a pinch of salt. Optionally, add a few drops of green food coloring for a vibrant color.
    - Mix well until fully combined.

6. **Cool and Chill:**
   - Let the mixture cool to room temperature, then cover and refrigerate for at least 4 hours or overnight until thoroughly chilled.
7. **Churn the Ice Cream:**
   - Once chilled, pour the Cucumber and Mint-infused custard into your ice cream maker and churn according to the manufacturer's instructions. This usually takes about 20-25 minutes, or until the ice cream reaches a soft-serve consistency.
8. **Freeze the Ice Cream:**
   - Transfer the churned Cucumber and Mint Ice Cream into a freezer-safe container.
   - Cover tightly with plastic wrap or a lid and freeze for at least 4 hours or until firm.
9. **Serve:**
   - Scoop and enjoy your creamy and refreshing homemade Cucumber and Mint Ice Cream!

This recipe offers a unique blend of cucumber's fresh essence and mint's cool flavor in a smooth and creamy dessert. It's perfect for hot summer days or as a palate-cleansing treat between courses. Adjust the sweetness and intensity of mint and cucumber according to your taste preferences for a personalized touch.

Pear and Blue Cheese Ice Cream

Ingredients:

- 2 ripe pears, peeled, cored, and diced
- 2 tablespoons lemon juice
- 1 tablespoon granulated sugar
- 1 cup (240ml) heavy cream
- 1 cup (240ml) whole milk
- 3/4 cup (150g) granulated sugar
- 4 ounces (about 110g) blue cheese, crumbled (such as Gorgonzola or Roquefort)
- 5 large egg yolks
- 1 teaspoon vanilla extract
- Pinch of salt

Instructions:

1. **Prepare the Pears:**
    - In a small bowl, toss the diced pears with lemon juice and 1 tablespoon of granulated sugar. Set aside.
2. **Prepare the Ice Cream Base:**
    - In a medium saucepan, combine the heavy cream, whole milk, and remaining granulated sugar over medium heat, stirring occasionally, until it begins to steam and small bubbles form around the edges. Do not let it boil.
3. **Prepare the Custard:**
    - In a separate bowl, whisk together the egg yolks until they are pale and slightly thickened.
    - Gradually whisk about 1/2 cup of the warm cream mixture into the egg yolks to temper them.
    - Slowly pour the tempered egg yolk mixture back into the saucepan with the remaining cream mixture, stirring constantly.
4. **Cook the Custard:**
    - Cook the mixture over medium-low heat, stirring constantly with a wooden spoon or heatproof spatula, until it thickens and coats the back of the spoon. This usually takes about 5-7 minutes. Do not let it boil.
5. **Incorporate Blue Cheese and Pears:**
    - Remove from heat and strain the custard through a fine-mesh sieve into a clean bowl to remove any cooked egg bits.

- Stir in the crumbled blue cheese, vanilla extract, and a pinch of salt until the cheese is melted and fully incorporated.
 - Fold in the prepared diced pears.
6. **Cool and Chill:**
 - Let the mixture cool to room temperature, then cover and refrigerate for at least 4 hours or overnight until thoroughly chilled.
7. **Churn the Ice Cream:**
 - Once chilled, pour the Pear and Blue Cheese-infused custard into your ice cream maker and churn according to the manufacturer's instructions. This usually takes about 20-25 minutes, or until the ice cream reaches a soft-serve consistency.
8. **Freeze the Ice Cream:**
 - Transfer the churned Pear and Blue Cheese Ice Cream into a freezer-safe container.
 - Cover tightly with plastic wrap or a lid and freeze for at least 4 hours or until firm.
9. **Serve:**
 - Scoop and enjoy your creamy and unique homemade Pear and Blue Cheese Ice Cream!

This recipe offers a surprising combination of flavors, with the sweetness of pears complementing the savory richness of blue cheese in a creamy ice cream base. It's a delightful dessert that showcases an unexpected pairing for adventurous taste buds. Adjust the amount of blue cheese and sweetness according to your taste preferences for a personalized twist.

Beetroot and Chocolate Ice Cream

Ingredients:

- 2 cups (480ml) heavy cream
- 1 cup (240ml) whole milk
- 3/4 cup (150g) granulated sugar
- 2 medium-sized beetroots, cooked, peeled, and grated (about 1 cup grated)
- 1/2 cup unsweetened cocoa powder
- 5 large egg yolks
- 1 teaspoon vanilla extract
- Pinch of salt

Instructions:

1. **Prepare the Beetroot Puree:**
    - Cook the beetroots until tender (you can boil, steam, or roast them). Once cooked, peel and grate them. Set aside.
2. **Prepare the Ice Cream Base:**
    - In a medium saucepan, combine the heavy cream, whole milk, and granulated sugar over medium heat, stirring occasionally, until it begins to steam and small bubbles form around the edges. Do not let it boil.
3. **Prepare the Custard:**
    - In a separate bowl, whisk together the egg yolks until they are pale and slightly thickened.
    - Gradually whisk about 1/2 cup of the warm cream mixture into the egg yolks to temper them.
    - Slowly pour the tempered egg yolk mixture back into the saucepan with the remaining cream mixture, stirring constantly.
4. **Incorporate Beetroot and Cocoa:**
    - Add the grated beetroot and unsweetened cocoa powder to the custard mixture in the saucepan.
    - Stir well to combine, ensuring the cocoa powder is fully incorporated.
5. **Cook the Custard:**
    - Cook the mixture over medium-low heat, stirring constantly with a wooden spoon or heatproof spatula, until it thickens and coats the back of the spoon. This usually takes about 5-7 minutes. Do not let it boil.
6. **Cool and Chill:**
    - Remove from heat and strain the custard through a fine-mesh sieve into a clean bowl to remove any cooked egg bits.

- Stir in the vanilla extract and a pinch of salt. Mix well.
7. **Cool and Chill:**
    - Let the mixture cool to room temperature, then cover and refrigerate for at least 4 hours or overnight until thoroughly chilled.
8. **Churn the Ice Cream:**
    - Once chilled, pour the Beetroot and Chocolate-infused custard into your ice cream maker and churn according to the manufacturer's instructions. This usually takes about 20-25 minutes, or until the ice cream reaches a soft-serve consistency.
9. **Freeze the Ice Cream:**
    - Transfer the churned Beetroot and Chocolate Ice Cream into a freezer-safe container.
    - Cover tightly with plastic wrap or a lid and freeze for at least 4 hours or until firm.
10. **Serve:**
    - Scoop and enjoy your creamy and flavorful homemade Beetroot and Chocolate Ice Cream!

This recipe offers a surprising blend of earthy sweetness from the beetroots combined with the rich, deep flavor of chocolate. It's a unique dessert that's sure to impress with its vibrant color and indulgent taste. Adjust the sweetness and intensity of cocoa according to your taste preferences for a personalized twist.

Fig and Honey Ice Cream

Ingredients:

- 1 cup (240ml) heavy cream
- 1 cup (240ml) whole milk
- 3/4 cup (150g) granulated sugar
- 1 cup fresh figs, diced (about 6-8 figs)
- 1/4 cup honey
- 5 large egg yolks
- 1 teaspoon vanilla extract
- Pinch of salt

Instructions:

1. **Prepare the Fig Puree:**
    - In a blender or food processor, puree the diced figs until smooth. Set aside.
2. **Prepare the Ice Cream Base:**
    - In a medium saucepan, combine the heavy cream, whole milk, and granulated sugar over medium heat, stirring occasionally, until it begins to steam and small bubbles form around the edges. Do not let it boil.
3. **Prepare the Custard:**
    - In a separate bowl, whisk together the egg yolks until they are pale and slightly thickened.
    - Gradually whisk about 1/2 cup of the warm cream mixture into the egg yolks to temper them.
    - Slowly pour the tempered egg yolk mixture back into the saucepan with the remaining cream mixture, stirring constantly.
4. **Incorporate Fig and Honey:**
    - Add the pureed figs and honey to the custard mixture in the saucepan.
    - Stir well to combine, ensuring the honey is fully incorporated.
5. **Cook the Custard:**
    - Cook the mixture over medium-low heat, stirring constantly with a wooden spoon or heatproof spatula, until it thickens and coats the back of the spoon. This usually takes about 5-7 minutes. Do not let it boil.
6. **Cool and Chill:**
    - Remove from heat and strain the custard through a fine-mesh sieve into a clean bowl to remove any cooked egg bits.
    - Stir in the vanilla extract and a pinch of salt. Mix well.

7. **Cool and Chill:**
   - Let the mixture cool to room temperature, then cover and refrigerate for at least 4 hours or overnight until thoroughly chilled.
8. **Churn the Ice Cream:**
   - Once chilled, pour the Fig and Honey-infused custard into your ice cream maker and churn according to the manufacturer's instructions. This usually takes about 20-25 minutes, or until the ice cream reaches a soft-serve consistency.
9. **Freeze the Ice Cream:**
   - Transfer the churned Fig and Honey Ice Cream into a freezer-safe container.
   - Cover tightly with plastic wrap or a lid and freeze for at least 4 hours or until firm.
10. **Serve:**
    - Scoop and enjoy your creamy and flavorful homemade Fig and Honey Ice Cream!

This recipe captures the natural sweetness of figs and the floral essence of honey in a smooth and creamy dessert. It's perfect for showcasing the flavors of fresh figs in a unique ice cream. Adjust the sweetness by varying the amount of honey according to your taste preferences for a personalized touch.

Toasted Coconut Ice Cream

Ingredients:

- 1 cup (240ml) heavy cream
- 1 cup (240ml) coconut milk
- 1 cup (240ml) whole milk
- 3/4 cup (150g) granulated sugar
- 1 cup shredded coconut (unsweetened)
- 5 large egg yolks
- 1 teaspoon vanilla extract
- Pinch of salt

Instructions:

1. **Toast the Coconut:**
    - Preheat your oven to 325°F (160°C).
    - Spread the shredded coconut evenly on a baking sheet lined with parchment paper.
    - Toast the coconut in the preheated oven for about 5-7 minutes, stirring occasionally, until it turns golden brown. Watch carefully to prevent burning. Remove from the oven and let it cool.
2. **Prepare the Ice Cream Base:**
    - In a medium saucepan, combine the heavy cream, coconut milk, whole milk, and granulated sugar over medium heat, stirring occasionally, until it begins to steam and small bubbles form around the edges. Do not let it boil.
3. **Prepare the Custard:**
    - In a separate bowl, whisk together the egg yolks until they are pale and slightly thickened.
    - Gradually whisk about 1/2 cup of the warm cream mixture into the egg yolks to temper them.
    - Slowly pour the tempered egg yolk mixture back into the saucepan with the remaining cream mixture, stirring constantly.
4. **Cook the Custard:**
    - Cook the mixture over medium-low heat, stirring constantly with a wooden spoon or heatproof spatula, until it thickens and coats the back of the spoon. This usually takes about 5-7 minutes. Do not let it boil.
5. **Incorporate Toasted Coconut:**

- Remove from heat and strain the custard through a fine-mesh sieve into a clean bowl to remove any cooked egg bits.
- Stir in the vanilla extract and a pinch of salt. Mix well.
- Fold in the toasted shredded coconut, reserving a small amount for garnish if desired.

6. **Cool and Chill:**
    - Let the mixture cool to room temperature, then cover and refrigerate for at least 4 hours or overnight until thoroughly chilled.
7. **Churn the Ice Cream:**
    - Once chilled, pour the Toasted Coconut-infused custard into your ice cream maker and churn according to the manufacturer's instructions. This usually takes about 20-25 minutes, or until the ice cream reaches a soft-serve consistency.
8. **Freeze the Ice Cream:**
    - Transfer the churned Toasted Coconut Ice Cream into a freezer-safe container.
    - Sprinkle the reserved toasted coconut on top if desired.
    - Cover tightly with plastic wrap or a lid and freeze for at least 4 hours or until firm.
9. **Serve:**
    - Scoop and enjoy your creamy and nutty homemade Toasted Coconut Ice Cream!

This recipe captures the rich, toasted flavor of coconut in a smooth and creamy dessert. It's perfect for coconut lovers and a delightful treat for any occasion. Adjust the sweetness by varying the amount of sugar according to your taste preferences for a personalized touch.

Brown Bread Ice Cream

Ingredients:

- 1 cup (240ml) heavy cream
- 1 cup (240ml) whole milk
- 3/4 cup (150g) granulated sugar
- 1 cup brown bread crumbs (from stale brown bread)
- 5 large egg yolks
- 1 teaspoon vanilla extract
- Pinch of salt
- 1/2 teaspoon ground cinnamon (optional)

Instructions:

1. **Prepare the Brown Bread Crumbs:**
   - If you don't have leftover stale brown bread crumbs, you can toast fresh brown bread slices in the oven until crispy, then process them into fine crumbs using a food processor or blender.
2. **Prepare the Ice Cream Base:**
   - In a medium saucepan, combine the heavy cream, whole milk, and granulated sugar over medium heat, stirring occasionally, until it begins to steam and small bubbles form around the edges. Do not let it boil.
3. **Prepare the Custard:**
   - In a separate bowl, whisk together the egg yolks until they are pale and slightly thickened.
   - Gradually whisk about 1/2 cup of the warm cream mixture into the egg yolks to temper them.
   - Slowly pour the tempered egg yolk mixture back into the saucepan with the remaining cream mixture, stirring constantly.
4. **Incorporate Brown Bread Crumbs:**
   - Add the brown bread crumbs to the custard mixture in the saucepan.
   - Optionally, add ground cinnamon for added flavor (if desired).
   - Stir well to combine.
5. **Cook the Custard:**
   - Cook the mixture over medium-low heat, stirring constantly with a wooden spoon or heatproof spatula, until it thickens and coats the back of the spoon. This usually takes about 5-7 minutes. Do not let it boil.
6. **Cool and Chill:**

- Remove from heat and strain the custard through a fine-mesh sieve into a clean bowl to remove any cooked egg bits.
- Stir in the vanilla extract and a pinch of salt. Mix well.

7. **Cool and Chill:**
   - Let the mixture cool to room temperature, then cover and refrigerate for at least 4 hours or overnight until thoroughly chilled.

8. **Churn the Ice Cream:**
   - Once chilled, pour the Brown Bread-infused custard into your ice cream maker and churn according to the manufacturer's instructions. This usually takes about 20-25 minutes, or until the ice cream reaches a soft-serve consistency.

9. **Freeze the Ice Cream:**
   - Transfer the churned Brown Bread Ice Cream into a freezer-safe container.
   - Cover tightly with plastic wrap or a lid and freeze for at least 4 hours or until firm.

10. **Serve:**
    - Scoop and enjoy your creamy and comforting homemade Brown Bread Ice Cream!

This recipe captures the nostalgic flavor of brown bread in a smooth and creamy dessert. It's perfect for those who appreciate unique flavors and want to try something different. Adjust the sweetness and cinnamon according to your taste preferences for a personalized touch.

Chai Spiced Ice Cream

Ingredients:

- 1 cup (240ml) heavy cream
- 1 cup (240ml) whole milk
- 3/4 cup (150g) granulated sugar
- 3-4 chai tea bags (or 3-4 tablespoons loose leaf chai tea)
- 5 large egg yolks
- 1 teaspoon vanilla extract
- 1/2 teaspoon ground cinnamon
- 1/4 teaspoon ground ginger
- 1/4 teaspoon ground cardamom
- 1/8 teaspoon ground cloves
- Pinch of ground black pepper (optional)
- Pinch of salt

Instructions:

1. **Infuse the Chai Flavors:**
    - In a medium saucepan, combine the heavy cream, whole milk, and granulated sugar over medium heat, stirring occasionally, until it begins to steam and small bubbles form around the edges. Do not let it boil.
    - Add the chai tea bags or loose chai tea (in a tea ball or infuser) to the cream mixture. Stir gently and let it steep for about 15-20 minutes over low heat to infuse the flavors. Taste occasionally to ensure it reaches your desired chai flavor intensity.
2. **Prepare the Custard:**
    - Remove the chai tea bags or infuser with loose tea from the cream mixture.
    - In a separate bowl, whisk together the egg yolks until they are pale and slightly thickened.
    - Gradually whisk about 1/2 cup of the warm chai-infused cream mixture into the egg yolks to temper them.
    - Slowly pour the tempered egg yolk mixture back into the saucepan with the remaining cream mixture, stirring constantly.
3. **Add Spices:**
    - Stir in the vanilla extract, ground cinnamon, ground ginger, ground cardamom, ground cloves, and a pinch of ground black pepper (if using). Mix well.

- Add a pinch of salt to enhance the flavors.
4. **Cook the Custard:**
   - Cook the mixture over medium-low heat, stirring constantly with a wooden spoon or heatproof spatula, until it thickens and coats the back of the spoon. This usually takes about 5-7 minutes. Do not let it boil.
5. **Cool and Chill:**
   - Remove from heat and strain the custard through a fine-mesh sieve into a clean bowl to remove any cooked egg bits and spices.
   - Let the mixture cool to room temperature, then cover and refrigerate for at least 4 hours or overnight until thoroughly chilled.
6. **Churn the Ice Cream:**
   - Once chilled, pour the Chai Spiced-infused custard into your ice cream maker and churn according to the manufacturer's instructions. This usually takes about 20-25 minutes, or until the ice cream reaches a soft-serve consistency.
7. **Freeze the Ice Cream:**
   - Transfer the churned Chai Spiced Ice Cream into a freezer-safe container.
   - Cover tightly with plastic wrap or a lid and freeze for at least 4 hours or until firm.
8. **Serve:**
   - Scoop and enjoy your creamy and aromatic homemade Chai Spiced Ice Cream!

This recipe captures the warm and comforting flavors of chai tea in a delightful frozen dessert. It's perfect for chai lovers looking to enjoy their favorite flavors in a new and refreshing way. Adjust the intensity of spices according to your taste preferences for a personalized chai experience.

Sloe Gin Ice Cream

Ingredients:

- 1 cup (240ml) heavy cream
- 1 cup (240ml) whole milk
- 3/4 cup (150g) granulated sugar
- 1/2 cup sloe gin
- 5 large egg yolks
- 1 teaspoon vanilla extract
- Pinch of salt

Instructions:

1. **Prepare the Ice Cream Base:**
    - In a medium saucepan, combine the heavy cream, whole milk, and granulated sugar over medium heat, stirring occasionally, until it begins to steam and small bubbles form around the edges. Do not let it boil.
2. **Incorporate Sloe Gin:**
    - Add the sloe gin to the cream mixture in the saucepan. Stir well to combine.
3. **Prepare the Custard:**
    - In a separate bowl, whisk together the egg yolks until they are pale and slightly thickened.
    - Gradually whisk about 1/2 cup of the warm cream mixture into the egg yolks to temper them.
    - Slowly pour the tempered egg yolk mixture back into the saucepan with the remaining cream mixture, stirring constantly.
4. **Cook the Custard:**
    - Cook the mixture over medium-low heat, stirring constantly with a wooden spoon or heatproof spatula, until it thickens and coats the back of the spoon. This usually takes about 5-7 minutes. Do not let it boil.
5. **Cool and Chill:**
    - Remove from heat and strain the custard through a fine-mesh sieve into a clean bowl to remove any cooked egg bits.
    - Stir in the vanilla extract and a pinch of salt. Mix well.
6. **Cool and Chill:**
    - Let the mixture cool to room temperature, then cover and refrigerate for at least 4 hours or overnight until thoroughly chilled.
7. **Churn the Ice Cream:**

- Once chilled, pour the Sloe Gin-infused custard into your ice cream maker and churn according to the manufacturer's instructions. This usually takes about 20-25 minutes, or until the ice cream reaches a soft-serve consistency.

8. **Freeze the Ice Cream:**
    - Transfer the churned Sloe Gin Ice Cream into a freezer-safe container.
    - Cover tightly with plastic wrap or a lid and freeze for at least 4 hours or until firm.
9. **Serve:**
    - Scoop and enjoy your creamy and sophisticated homemade Sloe Gin Ice Cream!

This recipe captures the unique flavors of sloe gin in a smooth and creamy dessert. It's perfect for special occasions or as a delightful treat for adults looking to enjoy a distinctive flavor profile in their ice cream. Adjust the amount of sloe gin according to your taste preferences for a more pronounced or subtle gin flavor.

Pistachio Ice Cream

Ingredients:

- 1 cup (240ml) heavy cream
- 1 cup (240ml) whole milk
- 3/4 cup (150g) granulated sugar
- 1 cup shelled pistachios, unsalted
- 5 large egg yolks
- 1 teaspoon vanilla extract
- Pinch of salt
- Green food coloring (optional, for a more vibrant green color)

Instructions:

1. **Prepare the Pistachio Paste:**
   - In a food processor or blender, grind the pistachios until they become a fine powder or paste. You may need to scrape down the sides occasionally to ensure even grinding. If the mixture is too dry, you can add a tablespoon of vegetable oil to help it blend into a smooth paste.
2. **Prepare the Ice Cream Base:**
   - In a medium saucepan, combine the heavy cream, whole milk, and granulated sugar over medium heat, stirring occasionally, until it begins to steam and small bubbles form around the edges. Do not let it boil.
3. **Incorporate Pistachio Paste:**
   - Add the pistachio paste to the cream mixture in the saucepan. Stir well to combine.
4. **Prepare the Custard:**
   - In a separate bowl, whisk together the egg yolks until they are pale and slightly thickened.
   - Gradually whisk about 1/2 cup of the warm cream mixture into the egg yolks to temper them.
   - Slowly pour the tempered egg yolk mixture back into the saucepan with the remaining cream mixture, stirring constantly.
5. **Cook the Custard:**
   - Cook the mixture over medium-low heat, stirring constantly with a wooden spoon or heatproof spatula, until it thickens and coats the back of the spoon. This usually takes about 5-7 minutes. Do not let it boil.
6. **Cool and Chill:**

- Remove from heat and strain the custard through a fine-mesh sieve into a clean bowl to remove any cooked egg bits.
- Stir in the vanilla extract and a pinch of salt. Mix well.
- Optionally, add a few drops of green food coloring for a more vibrant green color (if desired).

7. **Cool and Chill:**
   - Let the mixture cool to room temperature, then cover and refrigerate for at least 4 hours or overnight until thoroughly chilled.
8. **Churn the Ice Cream:**
   - Once chilled, pour the Pistachio-infused custard into your ice cream maker and churn according to the manufacturer's instructions. This usually takes about 20-25 minutes, or until the ice cream reaches a soft-serve consistency.
9. **Freeze the Ice Cream:**
   - Transfer the churned Pistachio Ice Cream into a freezer-safe container.
   - Cover tightly with plastic wrap or a lid and freeze for at least 4 hours or until firm.
10. **Serve:**
    - Scoop and enjoy your creamy and nutty homemade Pistachio Ice Cream!

This recipe captures the natural nuttiness of pistachios in a smooth and creamy dessert. It's perfect for pistachio lovers and a delightful treat for any occasion. Adjust the sweetness and intensity of pistachio flavor according to your taste preferences for a personalized touch.

Christmas Pudding Ice Cream

Ingredients:

- 1 cup (240ml) heavy cream
- 1 cup (240ml) whole milk
- 3/4 cup (150g) granulated sugar
- 1 cup crumbled Christmas pudding (homemade or store-bought)
- 5 large egg yolks
- 1 teaspoon vanilla extract
- 1/2 teaspoon ground cinnamon
- 1/4 teaspoon ground nutmeg
- 1/4 teaspoon ground cloves
- Pinch of salt
- Optional: 1/4 cup brandy or rum (for an extra festive touch)

Instructions:

1. **Prepare the Ice Cream Base:**
   - In a medium saucepan, combine the heavy cream, whole milk, and granulated sugar over medium heat, stirring occasionally, until it begins to steam and small bubbles form around the edges. Do not let it boil.
2. **Prepare the Christmas Pudding:**
   - Crumble the Christmas pudding into small pieces. If it's too dense, you can chop it finely or break it apart with your hands.
3. **Incorporate Christmas Pudding:**
   - Add the crumbled Christmas pudding to the cream mixture in the saucepan. Stir well to combine.
4. **Add Spices and Optional Brandy/Rum:**
   - Stir in the ground cinnamon, ground nutmeg, ground cloves, and a pinch of salt.
   - If using, add the brandy or rum for an extra festive touch. Mix well.
5. **Prepare the Custard:**
   - In a separate bowl, whisk together the egg yolks until they are pale and slightly thickened.
   - Gradually whisk about 1/2 cup of the warm cream mixture into the egg yolks to temper them.
   - Slowly pour the tempered egg yolk mixture back into the saucepan with the remaining cream mixture, stirring constantly.
6. **Cook the Custard:**

- Cook the mixture over medium-low heat, stirring constantly with a wooden spoon or heatproof spatula, until it thickens and coats the back of the spoon. This usually takes about 5-7 minutes. Do not let it boil.

7. **Cool and Chill:**
   - Remove from heat and strain the custard through a fine-mesh sieve into a clean bowl to remove any cooked egg bits and spices.
   - Stir in the vanilla extract. Mix well.

8. **Cool and Chill:**
   - Let the mixture cool to room temperature, then cover and refrigerate for at least 4 hours or overnight until thoroughly chilled.

9. **Churn the Ice Cream:**
   - Once chilled, pour the Christmas Pudding-infused custard into your ice cream maker and churn according to the manufacturer's instructions. This usually takes about 20-25 minutes, or until the ice cream reaches a soft-serve consistency.

10. **Freeze the Ice Cream:**
    - Transfer the churned Christmas Pudding Ice Cream into a freezer-safe container.
    - Cover tightly with plastic wrap or a lid and freeze for at least 4 hours or until firm.

11. **Serve:**
    - Scoop and enjoy your festive and flavorful homemade Christmas Pudding Ice Cream!

This recipe captures the essence of Christmas pudding in a creamy frozen dessert. It's perfect for holiday celebrations or anytime you want to enjoy the flavors of Christmas in a unique and delightful way. Adjust the amount of spices and optional brandy or rum according to your taste preferences for a personalized touch.

Bubblegum Ice Cream

Ingredients:

- 2 cups (480ml) heavy cream
- 1 cup (240ml) whole milk
- 3/4 cup (150g) granulated sugar
- 1/2 cup bubblegum flavor syrup or 10-12 bubblegum-flavored candies (like bubblegum balls)
- 5 large egg yolks
- 1 teaspoon vanilla extract
- Pinch of salt
- Pink or blue food coloring (optional)

Instructions:

1. **Prepare the Ice Cream Base:**
   - In a medium saucepan, combine the heavy cream, whole milk, and granulated sugar over medium heat, stirring occasionally, until it begins to steam and small bubbles form around the edges. Do not let it boil.
2. **Incorporate Bubblegum Flavor:**
   - If using bubblegum flavor syrup, add it to the cream mixture in the saucepan. Stir well to combine.
   - If using bubblegum candies, place them in a sturdy plastic bag and crush them into small pieces with a rolling pin or mallet. Add the crushed candies to the cream mixture. Stir well until the candies dissolve and the mixture is smooth.
3. **Add Food Coloring (if using):**
   - If desired, add a few drops of pink or blue food coloring to achieve a bubblegum-like color. Mix well.
4. **Prepare the Custard:**
   - In a separate bowl, whisk together the egg yolks until they are pale and slightly thickened.
   - Gradually whisk about 1/2 cup of the warm cream mixture into the egg yolks to temper them.
   - Slowly pour the tempered egg yolk mixture back into the saucepan with the remaining cream mixture, stirring constantly.
5. **Cook the Custard:**

- Cook the mixture over medium-low heat, stirring constantly with a wooden spoon or heatproof spatula, until it thickens and coats the back of the spoon. This usually takes about 5-7 minutes. Do not let it boil.

6. **Cool and Chill:**
   - Remove from heat and strain the custard through a fine-mesh sieve into a clean bowl to remove any cooked egg bits.
   - Stir in the vanilla extract and a pinch of salt. Mix well.

7. **Cool and Chill:**
   - Let the mixture cool to room temperature, then cover and refrigerate for at least 4 hours or overnight until thoroughly chilled.

8. **Churn the Ice Cream:**
   - Once chilled, pour the Bubblegum-infused custard into your ice cream maker and churn according to the manufacturer's instructions. This usually takes about 20-25 minutes, or until the ice cream reaches a soft-serve consistency.

9. **Freeze the Ice Cream:**
   - Transfer the churned Bubblegum Ice Cream into a freezer-safe container.
   - Cover tightly with plastic wrap or a lid and freeze for at least 4 hours or until firm.

10. **Serve:**
    - Scoop and enjoy your sweet and nostalgic homemade Bubblegum Ice Cream!

This recipe captures the fun and sweet flavor of bubblegum in a creamy and delightful dessert. It's perfect for kids and those who enjoy whimsical flavors. Adjust the intensity of bubblegum flavor and color according to your taste preferences for a personalized ice cream experience.

Rum and Raisin Ice Cream

Ingredients:

- 1 cup (240ml) heavy cream
- 1 cup (240ml) whole milk
- 3/4 cup (150g) granulated sugar
- 1 cup raisins
- 1/4 cup dark rum
- 5 large egg yolks
- 1 teaspoon vanilla extract
- Pinch of salt

Instructions:

1. **Prepare the Raisins:**
    - In a small bowl, soak the raisins in the dark rum. Let them soak for at least 1 hour, preferably longer (overnight if possible), until the raisins plump up and absorb the rum.
2. **Prepare the Ice Cream Base:**
    - In a medium saucepan, combine the heavy cream, whole milk, and granulated sugar over medium heat, stirring occasionally, until it begins to steam and small bubbles form around the edges. Do not let it boil.
3. **Prepare the Custard:**
    - In a separate bowl, whisk together the egg yolks until they are pale and slightly thickened.
    - Gradually whisk about 1/2 cup of the warm cream mixture into the egg yolks to temper them.
    - Slowly pour the tempered egg yolk mixture back into the saucepan with the remaining cream mixture, stirring constantly.
4. **Cook the Custard:**
    - Cook the mixture over medium-low heat, stirring constantly with a wooden spoon or heatproof spatula, until it thickens and coats the back of the spoon. This usually takes about 5-7 minutes. Do not let it boil.
5. **Incorporate Raisins and Rum:**
    - Remove the saucepan from heat. Strain the raisins from the rum (reserve the rum for later use).
    - Stir the plumped raisins into the custard mixture.
    - Stir in the vanilla extract and a pinch of salt. Mix well.
6. **Cool and Chill:**

- Let the mixture cool to room temperature, then cover and refrigerate for at least 4 hours or overnight until thoroughly chilled.
7. **Churn the Ice Cream:**
    - Once chilled, pour the Rum and Raisin-infused custard into your ice cream maker and churn according to the manufacturer's instructions. This usually takes about 20-25 minutes, or until the ice cream reaches a soft-serve consistency.
8. **Freeze the Ice Cream:**
    - Transfer the churned Rum and Raisin Ice Cream into a freezer-safe container.
    - Cover tightly with plastic wrap or a lid and freeze for at least 4 hours or until firm.
9. **Serve:**
    - Scoop and enjoy your creamy and boozy homemade Rum and Raisin Ice Cream!

This recipe captures the warm flavors of rum and the sweetness of plump raisins in a smooth and creamy dessert. It's perfect for adults looking to enjoy a classic ice cream with a hint of sophistication. Adjust the amount of rum and raisins according to your taste preferences for a more pronounced or subtle flavor.

Rocky Road Ice Cream

Ingredients:

- 1 cup (240ml) heavy cream
- 1 cup (240ml) whole milk
- 3/4 cup (150g) granulated sugar
- 1/4 cup unsweetened cocoa powder
- 1 cup mini marshmallows
- 1/2 cup chopped nuts (walnuts or almonds)
- 100g dark chocolate, chopped into small chunks
- 5 large egg yolks
- 1 teaspoon vanilla extract
- Pinch of salt

Instructions:

1. **Prepare the Ice Cream Base:**
    - In a medium saucepan, combine the heavy cream, whole milk, granulated sugar, and unsweetened cocoa powder over medium heat, stirring occasionally, until it begins to steam and small bubbles form around the edges. Do not let it boil.
2. **Prepare the Custard:**
    - In a separate bowl, whisk together the egg yolks until they are pale and slightly thickened.
    - Gradually whisk about 1/2 cup of the warm cream mixture into the egg yolks to temper them.
    - Slowly pour the tempered egg yolk mixture back into the saucepan with the remaining cream mixture, stirring constantly.
3. **Cook the Custard:**
    - Cook the mixture over medium-low heat, stirring constantly with a wooden spoon or heatproof spatula, until it thickens and coats the back of the spoon. This usually takes about 5-7 minutes. Do not let it boil.
4. **Cool and Chill:**
    - Remove from heat and strain the custard through a fine-mesh sieve into a clean bowl to remove any cooked egg bits.
    - Stir in the vanilla extract and a pinch of salt. Mix well.
5. **Cool and Chill:**
    - Let the mixture cool to room temperature, then cover and refrigerate for at least 4 hours or overnight until thoroughly chilled.

6. **Prepare the Mix-ins:**
   - While the ice cream base is chilling, prepare the mix-ins. Combine the mini marshmallows, chopped nuts, and dark chocolate chunks in a bowl.
7. **Churn the Ice Cream:**
   - Once chilled, pour the Rocky Road Ice Cream base into your ice cream maker and churn according to the manufacturer's instructions. This usually takes about 20-25 minutes, or until the ice cream reaches a soft-serve consistency.
8. **Add Mix-ins:**
   - During the last few minutes of churning, add the prepared mix-ins (marshmallows, nuts, and chocolate) to the ice cream maker. Churn briefly to evenly distribute them throughout the ice cream.
9. **Freeze the Ice Cream:**
   - Transfer the churned Rocky Road Ice Cream into a freezer-safe container.
   - Cover tightly with plastic wrap or a lid and freeze for at least 4 hours or until firm.
10. **Serve:**
    - Scoop and enjoy your indulgent homemade Rocky Road Ice Cream!

This recipe captures the classic flavors and textures of Rocky Road in a creamy and delicious ice cream. It's perfect for chocolate lovers and those who enjoy a bit of crunch and sweetness in their dessert. Adjust the amount of mix-ins according to your preference for a personalized Rocky Road experience.

Peanut Butter and Jelly Ice Cream

Ingredients:

- 1 cup (240ml) heavy cream
- 1 cup (240ml) whole milk
- 3/4 cup (150g) granulated sugar
- 1/2 cup smooth peanut butter
- 1/2 cup strawberry or grape jelly (or jam)
- 5 large egg yolks
- 1 teaspoon vanilla extract
- Pinch of salt

Instructions:

1. **Prepare the Ice Cream Base:**
   - In a medium saucepan, combine the heavy cream, whole milk, and granulated sugar over medium heat, stirring occasionally, until it begins to steam and small bubbles form around the edges. Do not let it boil.
2. **Incorporate Peanut Butter:**
   - Add the smooth peanut butter to the cream mixture in the saucepan. Stir well to combine until the peanut butter is fully melted and incorporated.
3. **Prepare the Custard:**
   - In a separate bowl, whisk together the egg yolks until they are pale and slightly thickened.
   - Gradually whisk about 1/2 cup of the warm cream mixture into the egg yolks to temper them.
   - Slowly pour the tempered egg yolk mixture back into the saucepan with the remaining cream mixture, stirring constantly.
4. **Cook the Custard:**
   - Cook the mixture over medium-low heat, stirring constantly with a wooden spoon or heatproof spatula, until it thickens and coats the back of the spoon. This usually takes about 5-7 minutes. Do not let it boil.
5. **Cool and Chill:**
   - Remove from heat and strain the custard through a fine-mesh sieve into a clean bowl to remove any cooked egg bits.
   - Stir in the vanilla extract and a pinch of salt. Mix well.
6. **Cool and Chill:**
   - Let the mixture cool to room temperature, then cover and refrigerate for at least 4 hours or overnight until thoroughly chilled.

7. **Prepare the Jelly Swirl:**
   - While the ice cream base is chilling, heat the jelly or jam in a small saucepan over low heat until it becomes slightly more liquid and easier to swirl.
8. **Churn the Ice Cream:**
   - Once chilled, pour the Peanut Butter Ice Cream base into your ice cream maker and churn according to the manufacturer's instructions. This usually takes about 20-25 minutes, or until the ice cream reaches a soft-serve consistency.
9. **Swirl in the Jelly:**
   - During the last few minutes of churning, drizzle the warm jelly or jam over the churned ice cream in the ice cream maker. Use a spoon or spatula to gently swirl it through the ice cream.
10. **Freeze the Ice Cream:**
    - Transfer the Peanut Butter and Jelly Ice Cream into a freezer-safe container.
    - Cover tightly with plastic wrap or a lid and freeze for at least 4 hours or until firm.
11. **Serve:**
    - Scoop and enjoy your creamy and nostalgic homemade Peanut Butter and Jelly Ice Cream!

This recipe captures the beloved flavors of peanut butter and jelly in a smooth and creamy dessert. It's perfect for all ages and a delightful treat that combines two classic flavors in a unique way. Adjust the amount of peanut butter and jelly according to your taste preferences for a personalized ice cream experience.

www.ingramcontent.com/pod-product-compliance
Lightning Source LLC
LaVergne TN
LVHW081556060526
838201LV00054B/1919